DATE DUE

THOUGHT

Gilbert Harman

THOUGHT

Princeton University Press
Princeton, New Jersey

Published by Princeton University Press,
Princeton and London

LCC: 72-4044
ISBN: 0-691-07188-8 (hardcover edition)
ISBN: 0-691-01986-X (paperback edition)

This book has been composed in Linotype Granjon
Printed in the United States of America by
Princeton University Press, Princeton, New Jersey

FIRST PRINCETON PAPERBACK Edition, 1974
Second Hardcover Printing, 1974
Third Printing, 1977

For Lucy

Kumfer 0803 0395 77 439682 16442 0160396

Preface

My conception of a person takes him to be a functional system of states and processes that possess representational characteristics by virtue of their role in the functional system. People differ from other animals in having language; that means that we can think in language, which gives us an advantage over the animals that cannot. On the other hand, not all human thought is in words. Our conception of ourselves in the world is more like a map than a story; and in perception our view of the world is more like a picture.

To the extent that thought is a matter of inference and reasoning, it is a matter of trying to increase the coherence of our total view. Coherence is a matter of explanation; that is why inference can involve deduction —not because there is such a thing as deductive inference, but because there is such a thing as deductive explanation.

Knowledge is acquired by inference that does not essentially involve anything false. Perceptual knowledge is thus based on actual inference; and knowledge retained in memory is continually reinferred.

These ideas emerge when skepticism is turned on its head and judgments about when we know are used to discover what inference is and when it occurs.

For advice and encouragement I am indebted to many teachers, students, colleagues, and friends, especially to Paul Benacerraf and Tom Nagel, Richard Jeffrey, Richard Rorty, C. G. Hempel, George Pitcher,

PREFACE

Saul Kripke, Robert Nozick, and Donald Davidson. The influence of the writings of W. V. Quine should be evident. None of these people is responsible for my blunders.

I have made use of portions of the following previously published material.

"Epistemology," to appear in Edward Carterette and Morton Friedman, *Handbook of Perception*. Academic Press: New York.

"Knowledge, Reasons and Causes," *The Journal of Philosophy* LXVII (1970): 841-855.

"Induction," in Marshall Swain (ed.), *Induction, Acceptance, and Rational Belief*. D. Reidel: Dordrecht, Holland (1970).

"Language, Thought, and Communication," to appear in a volume of *Minnesota Studies in the Philosophy of Science* to be edited by Keith Gunderson.

My work has been supported by the National Endowment in the Humanities, the National Science Foundation, and Princeton University.

Note to the third printing (1977): I have made substantive changes on pages 151 and 171 in response to comments by Ernest Sosa.

viii

Contents

THOUGHT

thought. . . .

1. The act or process of thinking; cogitation. 2. A product of thinking; idea; notion. . . .

The American Heritage Dictionary of the English Language. New York. Houghton Mifflin: 1969.

Chapter 1

Introduction

1. Radical skepticism

        Much of current epistemology (the theory of knowledge) in philosophy is best seen as a response to the thesis that we never have the slightest reason to believe anything. This radical skepticism must be distinguished from the more commonsensical idea that nothing can be known *for certain* and that we can never be *absolutely sure* of anything. Common sense assumes that practical certainty is possible even if absolute certainty is not. Radical skepticism departs from common sense and denies that even practical certainty is ever attainable. Indeed, it denies that anything is ever even the slightest bit more likely to be true than anything else.

    The problem is not that there are radical skeptics who need to be convinced that they are wrong. The problem is that an extremely natural line of argument seems to lead inevitably to radical skepticism. Common sense keeps us from accepting such a conclusion; but that leaves the philosophical problem of saying what goes wrong with the reasoning that seems to lead there. To repeat, the problem has not been to find an argument against skepticism, it has been to find out what is wrong with an argument for skepticism.

One such argument begins by asking how you know that the color red looks to someone else as it looks to you. Perhaps things that look red to you look green to him, things that look blue to you look orange to him, and similarly for other colors. If his spectrum is inverted compared with yours, there may be no way to discover it, since what is for you the experience of red he will call the experience of green. Even if he describes colors exactly as you do, there could still be a systematic difference between his and your experience of color. This suggests that you can have no reason to suppose that others see the world as you do rather than as does the man with an inverted spectrum.

Further reflection suggests that there is no reason to suppose that visual perception gives other people experiences that are anything like your visual experiences. Perhaps someone else has what would be for you auditory experiences. When he looks at the blue sky it is like what hearing middle C on the piano is for you. There seems to be no way to tell, since he would have been brought up to call that sort of experience the experience of blue. Indeed it is not clear that you have the slightest reason to suppose that others have anything you could recognize as experience. When others see things, their visual experience may be something you could not even imagine.

It might even be suggested that there is no reason to suppose that others have any experience at all. The suggestion is that, even if you could know that the people around you were made of flesh and blood, born of women, and nourished by food, they might, for all you know, be automatons in the sense that behind their elaborate

4

reactions to the environment there is no experience. But the suggestion is not merely that you do not *know* whether other people have any experience but also that you haven't the slightest reason to suppose they do.

Similarly, it might be suggested that you have not the slightest reason to believe that you are in the surroundings you suppose you are in, reading a book called *Thought*. It may look and feel to you as it would look and feel if you were in those surroundings, reading such a book. But various hypotheses could explain how things look and feel. You might be sound asleep and dreaming—or a playful brain surgeon might be giving you these experiences by stimulating your cortex in a special way. You might really be stretched out on a table in his laboratory with wires running into your head from a large computer. Perhaps you have always been on that table. Perhaps you are quite a different person from what you seem: you are a volunteer for a psychology experiment that involves having the experiences of someone of the opposite sex reading a book written in English, a language which in real life you do not understand. Or perhaps you do not even have a body. Maybe you were in an accident and all that could be saved was your brain, which is kept alive in the laboratory. For your amusement you are being fed a tape from the twentieth century. Of course, that is to assume that you have to have a brain in order to have experience; and that might be just part of the myth you are being given.

You might suppose that there are actually little differences among these hypotheses. After all, you have the same experiences on all of them. So you may feel that, no matter what is actually the case, everything will work out fairly well if you continue to act on the assumption that things are roughly what they seem. But that seems to go beyond your evidence. It may be that up until now everything has worked out well on the assumption that things are roughly what they seem to be. But what reason is there to suppose that things will continue to work out well on that assumption? An inductive inference is needed here: "Things have worked out well in the past; so they can be expected to work out well in the future." But how could you justify this use of induction? You might argue that, since inductions have generally worked out well in the past, you are entitled to expect them to work out well in the future. But that would be circular. You would be giving an inductive argument in order to defend induction.

Furthermore, do you really have any reason to suppose that things *have* worked out well in the past? You may seem to remember that they have. But how can you justify relying on your memory? Surely not on the grounds that your memory has been reliable in the past, for what reason do you have for thinking that it has been? The fact that you seem to remember that memory has been reliable in the past is irrelevant. You cannot legitimately appeal to memory to justify memory. You seem to have no reason to suppose that things have worked out well if and when in the past you have acted as if things are much as they seem.

Such reflections lead to the philosophical problems of other minds, the external world, induction, and memory. It is important that these problems are not simply whether we could ever know for sure or be absolutely certain of various matters. They are more radical: How is it possible that we should have the *slightest reason* to continue to believe as we do? How can there be more reason to believe what we do about the world than to believe anything else, no matter how incredible it may seem?

Recall that our interest in these problems is not that we want to be able to refute the radical skeptic. It is rather that we suppose that we often do have reasons to believe one thing rather than another and can sometimes even be practically certain, even if not theoretically certain, that we are right. Common sense tells us that something must be wrong with the arguments for radical skepticism. The philosophical problem is to spell out what is wrong.

Showing where the arguments for skepticism go wrong is philosophically interesting only to the extent that it tells us something interesting about reasons, inference, knowledge, and related matters. This book presents an account of the nature of thought that derives from an answer to skepticism. If the account is interesting, it is not because of light shed on skepticism but because of what is learned about these other things.

But before I present my own theory, I want to discuss a popular response to skepticism which ultimately leads nowhere.

2. The appeal to meaning

Some philosophical theories of knowledge appeal to meaning in the attempt to answer skepticism. The skeptical claim is said to be meaningless or false by definition. For example, *philosophical behaviorism* holds that statements about experience have the same meaning as do statements about behavior. On this view, the problem of the inverted spectrum is meaningless, since what it *means* for someone to see the world in the way that you see the world is that you and he are disposed to behave in the same way in the same perceptual situations. The supposition that you and he have roughly the same responses to color but that his spectrum is inverted with respect to yours would have no meaning.

According to philosophical behaviorism you can inductively discover someone's behavioral dispositions on the basis of purely behavioral evidence. You can know about his experience because you know that having certain experience is equivalent to having certain behavioral dispositions. This equivalence holds by virtue of the very definitions of words like "pain," "anger," "hunger," and so on. You know that the equivalence holds because you know what these words mean.

Similarly, a *phenomenalist* claims that statements about physical objects are equivalent in meaning to complex statements about possible sensory experience. According to a phenomenalist, to say that there is a typewriter on your desk is to say that under certain conditions it would look as if there were a typewriter on your desk, that certain experiences of seeming to type can be followed by experiences of seeming to read something freshly typed, and so forth. Phenomenalists argue that you know about these equivalences simply by virtue of knowing the meaning of statements about the external world. You use induction to justify statements asserting the possibility of sensory experience. Then you use the meaning equivalences to justify your views about the world.

It is true that philosophical behaviorism and phenomenalism appeal to induction as well as to meaning; but some philosophers have argued that inductive conclusions are themselves justified simply by virtue of the meaning of "justified." To reach a conclusion by induction is said to be almost by definition one of the ways you can justify a conclusion. Similarly, to say that something is probable is held to be to say that there are good reasons for it; in this context "good reasons" is supposed to mean "good inductive reasons." It is said to be "analytic" (i.e., true solely by virtue of meaning) that inductive reasons are good reasons, analytic that inductive conclusions are probably true, and analytic that inductive conclusions can be used to justify belief.

Some philosophers, not wishing to accept strict philosophical behaviorism, make a similar but weaker claim. These philosophers say that to understand the meaning of statements about someone else's experience you must realize that certain kinds of behavior will provide good, but not absolutely conclusive, evidence of that experience. According to these philosophers, it is part of the meaning of the word "pain" that certain behavior, such as moaning, is evidence that someone is in pain. Such evidence is said to be a "criterion" of pain. You are supposed to be able to know that others are in various psychological states because you can observe their behavior and know criteria for these states. You are supposed to know the criteria, not by virtue of any empirical investigation, but simply because you know the meaning of your words. So, for these philosophers, certain statements relating behavioral evidence and psychological states are analytic, true by virtue of meaning and known to be true by virtue of your knowledge of meaning.

Similarly, a philosopher who does not wish to accept phenomenalism can still argue that there are purely sensory criteria for statements about physical objects. Experience is evidence for claims about the external world, where the evidential relationship can be said to hold by virtue of meaning. It is said to be analytic that, if you seem to be seeing a blue book, that is adequate reason to believe that you are seeing a blue book, other things being equal. You are said to know an analytic truth like that because you know the meaning of the claim that you are seeing a blue book. You are said to be able to use experience as evidence about the external world because you know the meanings of your words.

The reliability of memory can also be defended by an appeal to meaning. The more radical view, corresponding to philosophical behaviorism and phenomenalism, is that statements about the past are equivalent in meaning to statements about present evidence. The weaker version has it that it is analytic of the notion of an apparent memory that apparent memories are good but not absolutely conclusive evidence for what is apparently remembered.

3. The revolt against meaning

According to philosophical behaviorism, statements about another person's experiences can be translated, without loss of meaning, into statements about his behavioral dispositions. Similarly, according to phenom-

enalism, statements about objects in the external world
can be translated without loss of meaning into statements about the possibility of one's own experience. In
either case, knowledge of truths about the experiences
of others or about objects in the world is supposed to be
made possible by knowledge of these translations, and
that knowledge is supposed to be available simply by
virtue of the fact that one knows the meanings of one's
words. Now, it was always embarrassing to philosophical behaviorism and to phenomenalism that no one was
ever able to give a single example of such a translation.
Lately it has become clear that the required sort of
translation is impossible. No single simple psychological
statement is equivalent in meaning to any nonpsycho-
logical statement that is purely about possible behavior.

A belief is not a simple behavioral disposition. At
best, it is a disposition to behave in certain ways *given
certain desires*. On the other hand, a desire is at best a
disposition to act in certain ways *given certain beliefs*.
This means that there can be no noncircular way to give
a purely behavioristic analysis of belief or desire. There
is no way to translate a simple statement about belief or
desire, without loss of meaning, into a statement that
speaks only of purely behavioral dispositions. The same
point holds for simple statements about other psychological states and about experiences.

Similarly, to say that there is a typewriter on your
desk is not to say, among other things, that under certain *purely experiential* conditions it would look to you
as if there were a typewriter on your desk. For these
conditions must include such things as that your eyes
are open, that nothing opaque intervenes between you

11

and the typewriter, that you have not just taken a hal-
lucinogenic drug, and so on. A statement of relevant
conditions must speak not only of possible experience
but also of things in the external world. There is no way
to translate simple statements about objects in the external world, without loss of meaning, into statements
that are solely about possible experience.

Psychological statements are to statements about behavioral dispositions, and statements about the external
world are to statements about possible experience, as
statements of theory are to statements of possible evidence. The failure of philosophical behaviorism and
phenomenalism illustrates the fact that individual theoretical statements cannot be translated without loss of
meaning into purely evidential statements. The point
goes back to Duhem, who noted that an individual theoretical statement does not have evidential consequences
all by itself but only in conjunction with other theoretical assumptions.

A more basic objection can be raised against any philosophical theories that attempt to answer skepticism by
appeal to meaning. Skepticism maintains that one never
has the slightest reason to believe one thing rather than
another. In attempting to meet skeptical arguments, one
eventually reaches a point at which (a) one wishes to
claim that certain evidence provides a good reason to
believe a particular conclusion but (b) one cannot offer
further grounds for this claim in response to any further
skeptical challenge. In another age, we might have said
that one can intuit the connection between evidence and
conclusion, but it is no longer felt that an appeal to intuition can explain one's knowledge of such a connec-

12

tion any better than an appeal to magic would. In this context analyticity seems to provide just what we are looking for. If the connection between evidence and conclusion holds by virtue of meaning, it would seem that one can know that the connection holds simply by virtue of knowing what one means. However, two questions immediately arise: (1) How does one know what one means? (2) How does knowledge of that meaning give one knowledge of the connection between evidence and conclusion? Unless these questions can be satisfactorily answered, the appeal to analyticity is as empty as an appeal to magic or to intuition.

Now, on the most plausible account of analyticity, the meaning of a person's words is determined by the way in which he intends to use those words. That a person can know what he means by his words would on this view be an instance of the more general point that a person can know what his intentions are. This account claims that sometimes these intentions can be expressed as an explicit definition, if one intends to use an expression solely as an abbreviation of another; and if one's intentions cannot be represented by an explicit definition, it is suggested that they can be expressed by "meaning postulates," which "implicitly define" the meaning of some of the expressions occurring in those postulates. For it is suggested that one intends to use one's words in such a way that the meaning postulates will be true.

There is obviously something to this account. The meaning of the expressions used to set forth any theory depend heavily on the basic principles of the theory. In explaining a theory by citing principles that give meaning to theoretical terms, we give our audience to under-

13

stand that we intend to use words in such a way that those principles will be true.

The problem is that intending that certain principles be true does not make them true, even when those principles give meaning to the terms used in stating them. What our words mean depends on *everything* we believe, on *all* the assumptions we are making. This is a consequence of the fact that we take another to mean the same by his words as we do only if this does not lead to the conclusion that certain of his beliefs are radically different from our own. In the latter case, if there is a relatively simple way to construe the other person's words so that he would then seem to have similar beliefs to our own, we will thus construe his words. This allows no room for a distinction between analytically true assumptions and others. For any assumption we make, it can happen that the best way to understand another person's view has him denying that assumption.

Applied to ourselves, the point becomes the Duhemian thesis that undermined philosophical behaviorism and phenomenalism. There is no way to divide our assumptions into those possibly disconfirmable by the evidence and others not susceptible to disconfirmation because they are analytically true. Our total view faces the evidence together as a whole. In the face of contrary evidence, some part of that view must be changed; and the history of science teaches that no part is immune to revision. Euclidean geometry, which was once taken as a paradigm of something which could be intuited to be true, was abandoned with the coming of relativity theory. Scientists do not hesitate to abandon a definition if that seems to be the best way to improve a going theory. And it has even been suggested that basic principles of logic might be refuted by appeal to quantum physics.

The appeal to analyticity was supposed to be an improvement over an appeal to magic or intuition. It now turns out to involve the supposition that assuming that something is true can make it true. We are not told how this is possible. We should have stuck with intuition and magic.

I will elaborate these sketchy remarks about meaning and analyticity below (in chapter six). I now want to say what use I would like to make of skepticism in order to shed light on the nature of thought.

4. Psychologism

Recall again that our aim is not to refute the skeptic but to learn from him. We are presented with a skeptical argument for a conclusion we do not accept. Although we do not accept the conclusion, we can still learn something from the skeptical argument, since any argument can be turned on its head. Since we suppose that skepticism is false, the fact that an argument leads to skepticism can be taken to show either that the argument is invalid or that one of its premises is false. If the argument is clearly valid, that fact can be used to demonstrate the falsity of one of the premises.

For example, how do you know that other people have the same sort of experience you have? Let us suppose that you infer that they do on the basis of their behavior. What justifies that inference? How can you rule out inverted spectra or experienceless automata? If such questions were approached directly, you would have to say, e.g., that inductive inference infers the simplest and most plausible explanation. Then you would have to show that the usual hypothesis is simpler and more plausible than the others. But what criteria of simplicity and plausibility could you appeal to in order to complete the argument?

The present suggestion is to turn the matter around. You are to use the fact that you accept a hypothesis as a sign that the hypothesis is simpler and more plausible than alternatives. The fact that you accept a hypothesis about other minds, as opposed to the inverted-spectrum hypothesis, shows that the usual hypothesis is simpler, less *ad hoc*, and more plausible. The suggestion is that, if we study this and other hypotheses we accept, we might begin to learn something about what makes a hypothesis better for us, i.e., better.

Similarly with knowledge of the external world. That you accept the hypothesis of the external world shows that it is reasonable to accept it. More specifically, as the result at least in part of your perceptual experience, you believe that you are now reading a book called *Thought*. Applying the suggested strategy, it follows that there is a warranted inference here. The hypothesis that you are now reading such a book provides the best explanation of your experience, given other things you believe. It provides a better explanation than the supposition that you are now dreaming or that you are being deceived by an evil computer. If we wish to learn more about this sort of inference to the best explanation, we must examine this and other cases of perceptual knowledge.

The old problem of induction was to justify the inductive inferences on which one's knowledge rests. What Goodman calls "the new riddle of induction" is to discover what the criteria of good inductive inference are. We are inclined to think that, if all observed A's are B's, that is a good reason to think that all A's are B's, especially if A's have been observed in various circumstances under various conditions. We have examined a great number of emeralds from various places and all of them have been found to be green. So we infer that all emeralds are green. But suppose one defines a predicate "grue" as follows: "x is grue at t" = "Either x is examined before the year 2000 A.D. and x is green at t or x is not examined before the year 2000 A.D. and x is blue at t." Notice that every emerald that has been examined has been found to be grue; and a great many emeralds have been examined from various places. What prevents the inference that all emeralds are grue? Something must be wrong with that conclusion since it conflicts with the earlier conclusion that all emeralds are green, at least for emeralds unobserved before the year 2000 A.D. For according to the first conclusion such emeralds are green, while according to the second they are blue. But how can the one hypothesis be any more supported by the evidence than the other?

Despite the large literature on this question, there seems to be little that can be said except that in fact we treat the inferences differently. The mind finds the one inference better than the other, even though in some abstract sense there is equal evidence for the two hypotheses. It is a fact about the mind that one hypothesis is, to use Goodman's term, more "projectible" than the other.

Goodman claims that projectibility is a function of past projection. Since "green" has figured in more actual inferences than "grue," his theory entails that the hypothesis with "green" in it is more projectible than the one with "grue." In fact, Goodman's theory may not go much beyond the nontheory of the previous paragraph. In order to find the principles of inductive inference, we must look to actual practice. The correct principles are those that account for the inferences that have actually been made. It follows that projectible predicates are those that get projected. If the mind treats one predicate differently from another, that will have had an effect on past projection. In the past we will have projected one but not the other. There is a correlation between projectibility and past projection. It makes little difference whether we say that past projection determines projectibility or that projectibility has been responsible for the past projection.

What is being suggested here is a kind of *psychologism*: the valid principles of inference are those principles in accordance with which the mind works. Of course, a simple statement like that is an idealization. Things can go wrong: we may fail to consider all the evidence; we can be biased; we commit fallacies. Still, the test of good inference is not whether it corresponds with rules that have been discovered *a priori*. The test can only be whether the inference seems right to someone who does his best to exclude things that can lead him astray.

Some philosophers criticize psychologism in logic on the grounds that it detracts from the certainty of logical truths and even makes them false, since some people reason invalidly. Some of this charge is answered by pointing out that the relevant rules concern the working of the mind when nothing goes wrong: how it works ideally. The rest of the complaint, that psychologism detracts from the certainty of logical truths, holds only for principles of deduction. The present topic is induction. Principles of deduction can be clearly stated, and they are probably more certain than any generalizations we might discover about the working of the mind. It would be wrong to take those principles to be principles about the working of the mind. But the principles of induction are not even known; so, of course, they cannot be clearly stated; and no statement of an inductive rule has the sort of certainty that attaches to the principles of deduction. There cannot be the same objection to identifying inductive principles with principles about the idealized working of the mind.

5. Knowledge and unconscious inference

Many philosophers reject the idea that knowledge is ultimately based on inference from data derived from immediate sensory experience. For example, they argue that ordinarily we are completely unaware of how things look, sound, smell, taste, feel, etc. It takes a great deal of training before a painter gets so that he can see things as they look. (How often do we notice that shadows have color?) But if we are rarely aware of what the sensory data are, how can our knowledge of the world be based on inference from such data?

Many philosophers would go on to say that in ordinary cases of (visual) perception we do not *infer* that something is there, we simply *see* that it is there. They would argue that you do not need to infer that there is printing on this page. "If you were blind or the lights were out, you might infer that there is printing on this page. You do not need to make an inference when you can see every word." They say that the word "inference" is misapplied here. It is clear that there is no conscious reasoning in ordinary perception. How could there be if we are not conscious of the premises of this reasoning? And philosophers have suggested that it is pure obscurantism to suggest that there is unconscious reasoning from unconscious premises, especially since such reasoning would have to be "instantaneous" (as soon as you saw this page you knew there was printing on it).

A difficulty with such arguments is that they require the assumption that we have an independent way to tell when inference has occurred and when it has not. It is not clear why that assumption is any more acceptable than the skeptical assumption that we know ahead of time what the valid principles of inference are. I suggest that the only way we can discover what those principles are is to discover what principles account for the inferences we actually make. Similarly, the only way to discover when a person makes inferences is to discover what assumptions about inference are needed to account for his knowledge. We can turn the arguments just considered on their heads. Knowledge of the world is based on inference. If there is knowledge of the world in perception, then there is inference in perception. If we are not conscious of the inference, then there is unconscious inference. If it would have had to be instantaneous, then inference takes no time. If we were not aware of the premises, then we can make inferences without being aware of the premises of those inferences. This line of reflection is supported by the following considerations.

In an important paper, Edmund Gettier demonstrates that the ordinary concept of knowledge cannot be defined as justified true belief. He describes a pair of situations in which a person believes something. In both situations, what he believes is true; and he is equally justified in believing as he does in the two situations. However, a speaker of English is inclined to say that the person would know something in the one situation but not in the other. Any such pair of situations can be called a *Gettier example*.

Here is a typical Gettier example. Consider a situation in which someone comes to know something by being told it by someone else. Then consider a situation like the first except that the speaker does not believe what he says. Suppose that, despite the speaker's intentions, what he says is true; and suppose that the hearer is as justified in believing the speaker in this case as in the first. Even so, anyone competent in English will be more inclined to say that the hearer comes to know something in the first situation than that he does in the second.

We might suggest that the hearer can infer the truth of what the speaker says only if he also infers that the speaker believes what he is saying. The hearer gains knowledge only if everything he must infer is true. Since the speaker believes what he is saying in the first situation but not in the second, the hearer can come to know in the first but not the second situation. If such a suggestion is correct, Gettier examples can be used to discover something about inference. The principles of inference must account for the fact that the hearer can infer that what the speaker says is true only if he also infers that the speaker believes what he is saying.

I shall argue in chapter ten that a person is to infer the most coherent explanatory account that makes the least change in his antecedent beliefs. For example, the hearer infers that the speaker says what he does because he believes it, and believes it because he saw it happen. Part of the reason for accepting this theory of inference is that it provides an answer to radical skepticism. We are justified in continuing to believe something unless we have a special reason to change our minds. The hypotheses the skeptic discusses are not equally reasonable, since only one of them is already believed.

Now, it is interesting to notice that there are Gettier examples involving simple perceptual knowledge. A person may see that there is a candle a few feet in front of him. Another person may be equally justified in believing that there is a candle in front of him and he may be right too, although a mirror intervenes between the second person and his candle so that what he sees is the reflection of a different candle off to one side. A speaker of English is inclined to say that the first perceiver knows that there is a candle in front of him but the second does not, even though both have equally justified true belief.

I shall argue that we cannot easily account for perceptual Gettier examples unless we assume that even simple perceptual knowledge is based on inference. In that case, the perceiver can be assumed to infer that the explanation of there seeming to be a candle ahead is that he is seeing a candle there. He comes to know that there is a candle there only if he is right about why it seems to him that there is a candle there.

That perception involves inference comes as no surprise to a perceptual psychologist who studies the cues used in depth perception. What is interesting is the connection between that idea and an investigation into the ordinary use of the word "know." In this book I propose to take the ordinary concept of knowledge seriously. I shall attempt to develop a theory that accounts for the ordinary use of the word "know" and, in the process, has something to say about inference, reasoning, perception, explanation, and many other topics.

Chapter 2

Reasons and Reasoning

1. Believing for reasons

Let us begin by considering when reasons would ordinarily be said to give a person knowledge. Consider the following example. Albert believes that he will not pass his ethics course. He has excellent reasons for believing this, because he failed the midterm examination, he has not been able to understand the lectures for several weeks, and the instructor is known to fail a high percentage of his students. Despite the fact that, like many other students, Albert does not appreciate the force of such reasons, he is influenced by something else. During a class discussion early in the term, he gave an emotional speech in favor of existentialism; and, although his instructor said nothing at the time, he seems to advocate linguistic analysis. Albert reasons that, since analytic philosophers hate existentialists, the instructor will remember his remarks, hold them against him, and fail him in the course.

In such a case, Albert cannot be said to know that he will fail. I put the point this way, because it seems misleading to say that Albert does not know that he will fail. Just as it would be misleading to say of Albert either that he realizes he will fail or that he does not realize that he will fail, it would also be wrong to say either that he knows that he will fail or that he does not know that he will fail.

We can account for our inability to say either "knows" or "does not know" by distinguishing presupposition from assertion. In the present context, when we say that Albert knows or does not know that he will fail, we assert that Albert thinks, or does not think, that he will fail. We presuppose (a) that Albert will fail and (b) that, if he should think that he will fail, he would know that he will fail. Since presupposition (b) is false, we should say neither that Albert knows nor that he does not know.

Other uses of "know" have different presuppositions. Sometimes we do not presuppose the truth of what is said to be or not to be known. For example, I might discuss with a representative of the tobacco industry whether scientists know that cigarettes cause lung cancer. I assert and he denies that the scientific evidence establishes a particular conclusion. We both presuppose that, if the evidence establishes or were to establish the conclusion, the scientists know or would know that cigarettes cause lung cancer.

This distinction between presupposition and assertion helps to explain our occasional difficulty in reaching agreement about whether various examples are examples of knowledge. Someone might point to the fact that we should not say Albert does not know that he will fail. This, it might be suggested, shows that Albert does know after all. We can avoid the latter conclusion if we distinguish presupposition from assertion.

So we may conclude that even though Albert believes that he will fail and has excellent reasons for believing this, he is not justified in believing it, and he cannot be said to know that he will fail. The moral is that reasons for believing something must not be confused with reasons for which one believes. Reasons for which one believes are relevant to whether one is justified in believing as one does. Reasons for believing something are not relevant unless they are also reasons for which one believes.

2. Telling one's reasons

I want to say what it is for certain reasons to be reasons for which a person believes something and what it is for certain reasons to be reasons which give a person knowledge. A familiar suggestion is that relevant reasons are those a person would offer if asked to justify his belief. This suggestion cannot be correct. Albert may offer good reasons, not because he thinks that they are any good, but because he thinks that they will convince his audience. Such reasons are not reasons for which he believes as he does, nor can they give him knowledge.

Suppose Albert's adviser asks him to defend his view that he will fail the ethics course. Albert may know that his adviser believes that grades are a good indication of how well a student has mastered the subject and does not believe that they are determined by whether a teacher likes a student. Furthermore, Albert may doubt that his adviser would think an analytic philosopher might dislike a student just because the student favored existentialism. So Albert might not tell his adviser what are, in his opinion, the real reasons why he is going to fail. Instead he might speak of his poor performance on the midterm examination, his inability to follow the lectures, and the reputation of his instructor as a severe grader. He may not think that these considerations are of any importance; but he may believe that his adviser will find them convincing. In such a case, reasons put forward to justify a belief are not reasons for which it is believed.

Nor is the analysis to be rescued by requiring that Albert be sincere. Being asked to justify his belief might lead Albert to reassess his reasons; and that could lead him for the first time to appreciate his good reasons. He might begin to see the significance of his performance on the midterm examination, his inability to understand the lectures, and the instructor's reputation. Having believed for some time that he would fail, he might only then come to believe this for the good reasons he then states; and only then could he be said to know that he is going to fail. It is possible that if he has not yet been asked to justify his belief, he does not believe it for good reasons and he cannot be said to know that it is true; yet if he were asked to justify his belief, he could at that point come up with good reasons, reasons that would at that point give him knowledge.

It follows that reasons for which a person believes something cannot be identified with reasons he would sincerely offer if asked to justify his belief. Nor can reasons which give a person knowledge be identified with reasons he would thus sincerely offer if asked to.

But there is a more basic objection to the suggestion that relevant reasons are those a person would offer if asked. The suggestion rests on an identification of *reasons* with *conscious reasons*, where a man's conscious

27

reasons are those he can tell us about. To equate reasons for which he believes something with reasons he can tell us about is to assume that reasons for which he believes something are conscious reasons; and that assumption is a mistake. The reasons for which people believe things are rarely conscious. People often believe things for good reasons, which give them knowledge, without being able to say what those reasons are. We can easily imagine Albert unaware of his real reasons for believing that he will fail. We might suppose (contrary to suppositions made so far) that Albert really did appreciate the significance of his failure to pass the midterm, his inability to understand the lectures, and the reputation of the instructor. That led him to realize that he would fail; but, not wishing to suppose that he is incompetent, he preferred to think he would fail because of the instructor's dislike for him. In such a case Albert would not have been consciously aware of the real reasons for his belief, although he would have known that he would fail.

The same point follows from the fact that in most cases we cannot say in any detail why we believe as we do. At best we can give a vague indication of reasons we find convincing. It is only in rare cases that we can tell a person's detailed reasons from what he can say about them. Indeed it is doubtful that we can ever fully specify our reasons.

This will not seem obvious if we think only of deductive reasons: reasons that deductively entail a conclusion. Deductive "reasoning" can be fully specified; hence the idea that "deductive reasons" can be fully specified. Not so for inductive reasons. It is doubtful that anyone has ever fully specified an actual piece of inductive reasoning, since it is unlikely that anyone could specify the relevant total evidence in any actual case. The difficulty is not simply that there is so much relevant evidence but also that one cannot be sure that various things should or should not be included in the evidence. One cannot always be sure what has influenced one's conclusion. (I return to the difference between induction and deduction in chapter ten, sections 1-3.)

Reflection on examples suggests that coming to believe something for certain reasons has something to do with why one comes to believe it. The reasons for which Albert believes as he does seem to depend on the explanation of his coming to believe as he does. These reasons can involve either his theory that the teacher dislikes him or his realization that he is not doing well in the course. What distinguishes these cases cannot be Albert's thinking that certain reasons are his reasons. His views about what his reasons are can be the same in both cases. Instead, the difference seems to lie in *why* he believes as he does. In imagining that he believes as he does for reasons involving his realization that he is philosophically incompetent, we ascribe to his belief a different explanation from that we ascribe to it when we say that he really believes as he does for reasons involving his theory that the instructor has it in for existentialists. More generally, it is difficult to see how to imagine a difference in the reasons for which people believe as they do without imagining a difference in the explanation of why they believe as they do. The same point holds for our own case. When we wonder whether a consideration represents one of our reasons, we wonder whether that consideration influenced our conclusion. But that is to wonder whether it has anything to do with why we believe as we do and, therefore, with the explanation of our belief.

3. Explanation by reasons

In order to say what sort of explanation this is, we must distinguish two cases, that in which one originally comes to believe something and that in which one continues to believe something although one's reasons change. When a person first comes to believe something, why he believes it appears to be a function of how he came to believe it. The differences we imagine in imagining the two possibilities concerning Albert are differences in how Albert comes to believe that he will fail. But it is not in general true that the reasons for which one believes as one does are simply a matter of how one came to believe what one believes. When the reasons why one believes something change, the reasons for which one believes as one does also change. In that case, the explanation of why one believes as one does has changed and is no longer simply a matter of how one came to believe as one does.

At this point it is useful to note an important connection between reasons and reasoning. To specify a man's reasons is always to specify reasoning that leads to his conclusion. It is never enough simply to specify premises from which the conclusion may be inferred. We must also indicate how the conclusion is obtained from those premises. Two people starting from the same premises and reaching the same conclusion can go by different routes; as a result, they may believe the conclusion for different reasons. If the first man's reasoning is sound but the second's is not, the first will believe for good reasons while the second believes for bad reasons. One man can know while a second fails to know, even though they both start from the same premises and reach the same conclusion.

This indicates that a person's reasons are a function of his reasoning and that to say that a man believes something for certain reasons is to say that he believes it as the result of certain reasoning.

A familiar objection is that one is rarely aware of the relevant reasoning. But awareness is not important. To claim that one believes something for certain reasons only if one believes it as the result of certain reasoning is not to claim that one is aware that one believes something for certain reasons only if one is aware that one believes it as the result of relevant reasoning. And, after the work of Freud and Wittgenstein, it is no longer plausible to equate mental processes with conscious processes. If reasoning is in some sense a mental process, still it is rarely a conscious process. I have already noted that even when one is aware of one's reasoning, one is rarely able to tell exactly what considerations have influenced one's conclusion (cf. chapter eleven, section 3).

It is, by the way, interesting to note that reasoning can explain a man's knowledge even though it does not explain his corresponding belief.[1] Larry's wife Mabel has been accused of embezzling a large sum of money

[1] Here I am indebted to Keith Lehrer. See also Lehrer (1971).

from the bank in which she works as a teller. Larry loves Mabel dearly and thinks he knows her as well as anyone can know anyone else. He cannot believe that Mabel could have embezzled money. In order to save her from jail he sets out to prove Mabel's innocence by finding the real embezzler. He is successful and is able to uncover evidence sufficient to prove that the bank manager took the money. The evidence Larry collects supports his belief in Mabel's innocence and it can give him knowledge where before he had only firm conviction. However, it need not add any force to his conviction, which may be already so strong that nothing could shake it. Larry's new reasons explain his knowledge but not his belief that Mabel is innocent. (The conditions under which reasoning explains knowledge are discussed in chapter ten, section 5.)

We can explain someone's belief or knowledge by citing reasoning. In giving this sort of explanation by reasons, we do not assume that reasoning is a causal or deterministic process. That a man accepts certain premises does not determine that he will accept the conclusion. That those premises provide a good reason for accepting the conclusion does not insure that he will think up the reasoning which shows this. It may be true that one step of reasoning is in fact part of the cause of the next. But we make no such causal assumption when we cite a person's reasoning as the explanation of his belief. Our explanation can be true even if the causal assumption is not.

In the next chapter I shall argue that explaining why someone believes something is like explaining why a nondeterministic automaton is in a particular state. Various moves are always possible. We do not assume that it is determined which move will be made. We do not even assume that various moves are more or less probable. We only assume that they are possible. We can explain how we got to wherever it was we got to without implying that we had to get there.

Chapter 3

Mental Processes

In order to say more about thinking and reasoning I must now sketch a general theory of mental processes. This will make it clearer why what is mental is not at all the same as what is conscious. It will also permit me to say more about psychological explanation so that I can show how reasons can figure in the explanation of belief. I will defend a kind of functionalism which defines mental states and processes in terms of their roles in a functional system.

As far as inference is concerned, its function in giving us knowledge proves all important. That justifies the strategy, adopted in chapter one and exploited in chapters seven through twelve, by virtue of which I appeal to intuitions about knowledge to learn something about reasoning rather than vice versa.

Chapters four, five, and six discuss mental states, specifically their representational character and how that is related to the meaning of sentences. Functionalism is relevant there, since representational character and meaning will be seen to depend on function.

Much of this book depends on the ensuing theory of representation. Inference, conceived in the most general way, is a process that modifies the way we represent the world. Some of this representation is linguistic, as when we think in words; some is not, as in perceptual experience. An oversimplified account of this distinction can support the confused ideas about analytic truth deplored in chapter one and decisively repudiated in chapter six. The distinction is also relevant to the account of perceptual knowledge in chapter eleven.

1. Dualism

We are tempted to take conscious experience to be paradigmatically mental. Moreover, a headache, an itch, a sudden thought, a feeling of joy, a pang of longing, or the awareness of a beautiful blue may seem very different from any physical process such as the excitation of nerve ends in the brain. We have a direct acquaintance with experiences and mental processes in general that, it seems, we can never have with physical processes. Some such line of thought may persuade us to accept a form of dualism—the idea that mental and physical processes are basically and irreducibly different. We may even decide that there must be two basic kinds of *substances*, minds and bodies.

Such dualism tends naturally to a form of dualistic interactionism—the theory that there is a causal interaction between the mental and the physical. For in visual perception, physical processes involving reflected light cause visual experiences and thoughts about what is seen. And mental processes culminating in decisions to undertake a particular course of action affect the movement of one's body.

35

But dualistic interactionism conflicts with the plausible and widely held view that in some sense there are no facts over and above the purely physical facts. Scientists believe that the totality of physical facts completely determines all other facts and that, in particular, all mental processes are completely determined by whatever physical processes there are. (This is not to say that physical processes themselves are causally determined by prior physical processes. According to quantum theory, that sort of determinism is false. But it is compatible with quantum theory to suppose that physical processes completely determine all nonphysical processes.) This rules out a mental realm distinct from a physical realm with which it occasionally interacts.

True, the idea that physical facts determine everything else is more trivial than may at first appear. If scientists discover a phenomenon that has physical effects but is not reducible to phenomena currently accepted as physical, they classify the new phenomenon as a new *physical* phenomenon. Some years ago, physical phenomena were thought to be entirely a matter of the movements of particles. When electromagnetic phenomena had to be accommodated, scientists did not suggest that there were two interacting but distinct realms, the physical and the electromagnetic. Instead they modified their conception of the physical to include electromagnetic phenomena.

But should we then suppose, e.g., that the mind is something like a *mental field*, different from and not reducible to other physical phenomena but interacting with them? Although the suggestion might be defended

36

by appeal to alleged instances of mental telepathy, ESP, and psychokinesis, along with speculation that free choice operates in the area of quantum indeterminacy, that would really be to indulge in a kind of crackpot science. We should be able to understand mental processes without such hypotheses.

Furthermore, the idea that free will requires an underlying neurophysiological indeterminism, perhaps at the quantum level, is a philosophical mistake. It is true that explanation by reasons, whether of beliefs or decisions, is *non*deterministic. But, as I will argue in detail below, that does not mean that such explanation involves any commitment to an underlying *in*determinism. Explanation by reasons is compatible with an underlying indeterminism and with an underlying determinism. It involves no commitment either way.

Aside from worries about free will, the main support of dualism is the idea that one has a direct acquaintance with experiences and mental processes which one cannot have with respect to merely physical processes. It is true that when one has a headache there is an important sense in which one can be aware of an experience without being aware of a physical process. For one can be aware *that* a headache is occurring without being aware that a physical process is occurring. But that shows nothing. That one is unaware that a headache is a physical process by no means establishes that a headache is not a physical process. When one is aware of a headache there are many facts about the headache of which one is unaware. Facts about awareness provide no real evidence for dualism.

37

2. *An identity theory*

On the other hand, there are difficulties in the suggestion that a headache might just *be* a particular neurophysiological process, e.g., a certain pattern of electrical discharges in the brain; and similarly for other experiences and mental processes. For, if the suggestion is that in general for there to be a headache *is* for there to be such and such a pattern of electrical discharges—so that wherever there is the appropriate pattern of electrical discharges there is *ipso facto* a headache—then we must ask about relevant patterns of electrical discharge that do not happen to occur in a living brain but occur, e.g., in a cloud during an electrical storm or in something struck by lightning. Are such occurrences also experiences of headaches, occurring apart from the other sorts of experiences that go to make up the life of a person or animal? If we think *yes*, we will be led perhaps to suppose that experiences are all around, occurring occasionally in trees, etc. And that is to be led again into a kind of mystical crazy science not appropriate to the present investigation. But if we agree that it is only in the context of a living brain that such occurrences *are* experiences of headaches, then we must say why that is so. How can exactly the same sort of physical process *be* a conscious experience when it occurs in one context but not when it occurs in another?

Further reflection along these lines shows that an identity theory is wrong if it always identifies a mental process or experience with the same sort of physical process. For suppose that neurophysiologists were to decide that a certain area of the brain serves as a "pain center." On the identity theory, different patterns of electrical activity in this area would *be* different sorts of pains. But now suppose that a brain surgeon removes the pain center in someone's brain and replaces it with a plastic transitorized construction that is functionally equivalent, although its inner workings are different from those in the natural brain center. The artificial replacement accepts the same input electrical pulses and emits the same output pulses that the natural brain center would. But patterns of electrical activity characteristic of various sorts of pains in the natural pain center do not occur at all in the artificial pain center. Quite different patterns occur instead. Could a person with an artificial pain center feel pain? Given the functional equivalence of the artificial to the natural pain center, he will occasionally act as if he is in pain and, indeed, say that he is in pain—(so that it would be difficult to convince *him* that he is not in pain). But if such a person could have a headache, then the occurrence of a headache cannot be simply identified with the occurrence of the specified pattern of electrical activity in the pain center. It follows that variously different physical processes, involving variously different physical substances, may be the underlying physical bases for the same experiences and mental processes. A general identity theory, according to which a particular sort of mental process is always the same as a particular sort of physical process, is mistaken.

Of course, the idea that scientists might construct an artificial pain center is, so far, just a myth. But the point of the myth is a valid one. One person's brain differs in many ways from another's. There is no reason to suppose that similar neurophysiological processes in different people underlie similar mental processes.

3. Behaviorism

A behaviorist theory would provide a way out of the preceding difficulty. Behaviorism analyzes mental life in terms of dispositions to behave in various ways in various circumstances. In chapter one I discussed a form of the theory according to which behavioristic analyses hold by virtue of meaning. But behaviorism can also be taken simply to offer an account of the nature of mental processes that makes no claims about the meaning of words used to describe these processes.

A behaviorist says that a mental state is a relatively long-term disposition to behave in certain ways. A belief that it will rain is a disposition to do such things as carry an umbrella; a desire for money is the disposition to perform acts that tend, other things equal, to get one money; intelligence is a general disposition to do the appropriate thing to obtain that which one is tending toward; good humor is the disposition to respond well to circumstances and the actions of others, etc. Similarly, an experience is a short-term behavioral disposition. A pain is, e.g., a disposition to soothe the painful spot (coupled with a disposition to complain). Finally, a mental process is a change in the dispositions characterizing mental states and experiences. For example, theoretical reasoning is a change (or a series of changes) in belief, i.e., a change in certain relatively long-term dispositions to act in various ways.

Different underlying physical mechanisms can be responsible for exactly the same dispositions. According to behaviorism, replacing a person's pain center with an artificial model cannot affect his capacity to feel pain unless it interferes with his dispositions to respond in various ways in certain situations. So behaviorism easily accounts for the facts that undermine a crude identity theory.

Nevertheless, the objection to behaviorism I mentioned in chapter one still applies. There is no noncircular way to specify the relevant dispositions. For they are dispositions to act in certain ways given certain situations; and the relevant situations essentially include beliefs about the situation and desires concerning it. What a man will do if he hits his thumb with a hammer depends on who he believes is watching and what desires he has concerning his relationship to the watchers. But beliefs are dispositions to act in certain ways only given certain desires, whereas desires are dispositions to act in certain ways only given certain beliefs. A belief that it will rain will be manifested in the carrying of an umbrella only in the presence of a desire not to get wet; and the desire for money will manifest itself in acts that tend to get one money only if one believes that those acts will get one money. Since even in theory there is no noncircular way to specify relevant dispositions in pure behavioral terms, behaviorism cannot provide an adequate account of mental processes and experience.

4. A modified Ramsey method

I mentioned in chapter one that the connection between a man's behavior and the inner psychological states and processes responsible for it is like the connection between evidence and a theory that explains the evidence. The failure of behaviorism is a special case of the failure of theoretical reductionism. Theoretical facts cannot be identified with purely evidential facts.

It is useful to think of commonsense psychological views as forming a more or less complete theory. Crudely put, the theory says that desires and beliefs together influence what we do, that perception modifies belief in certain ways, that desires can result from deprivation of food and water, that reasoning can bring about changes in belief and desire, and so forth. Various desires and beliefs are here taken to be theoretical states postulated to explain behavior.

Ramsey suggested that references to theoretical states and processes be replaced with existentially quantified variables in the overall theory. Ramsey's method applied to commonsense psychology yields the theory that *there are states and processes* related in certain specified ways to each other and to perception, deprivation, and action, etc.

If there are states and processes appropriately interrelated, they can be identified with beliefs, desires, reasoning, and so forth. But our reflections so far cast doubt on the existence of such states and processes. We have just seen that dispositional states and modifications of these states will not do the trick. And earlier we saw that particular sorts of mental states or processes cannot be identified with always the same physical states and processes. Yet if we were to decide that mental states and processes were *sui generis* and not constituted by neurophysiological states and processes, we would be flying in the face of scientific good sense. For then we would have returned to a form of dualism.

The solution to this problem is to modify Ramsey's method for handling theoretical terms. Ramsey has us quantify over the theoretical states first: *There are states and processes such that for any person. . . .* But we have learned that the physical states and processes underlying particular mental states and processes in one person can be different from those underlying the mental states and processes of a different person or even of the same person at a different time. The solution is to change the order of the quantifiers: *For any person (at a particular time) there are states and processes. . . .* Any person has states and processes in him related in certain specified ways to themselves and to perception, deprivation, action, etc. Those are his mental states and processes. On the other hand, it need not be true (and almost certainly is not true) that there are particular states and processes which in every person are related in the relevant ways, since the relevant states and processes almost certainly vary from person to person and in any one person over time.

So a kind of identity theory can be accepted. Instances of mental states and processes are instances of physical states and processes, although different instances of the same mental states and processes need not be instances of the same physical states and processes. But more must be said to clarify this account.

5. Functionalism

A psychological theory, commonsense or otherwise, may usefully be interpreted as a psychological model.

43

To have a theory of another person's psychological makeup is to have a model of the workings of his mind. We have somewhat different models for different people, although all psychological models share certain structural features.

A psychological model represents a more or less rigorously specified device that is intended to be able to duplicate the relevant behavior of a person. If the device is sufficiently described, it should be realizable as a robot or, as I shall say, an automaton.

An abstract automaton is specified by its program. The program indicates possible reactions to input, how internal states plus input can yield other internal states, and how internal states and input can lead to various sorts of output. In a psychological model, input can represent the effect of perception and output can represent intentional action.

An abstract automaton may be nondeterministic or deterministic, depending on its program. If the program implies that any combination of internal states and input always has a unique result, the program specifies a deterministic automaton. If some combinations might be followed by any of a number of different results, the program specifies a nondeterministic automaton. We shall see in section 7 that automata serving as psychological models should be nondeterministic.

The same abstract automaton can be instantiated in quite different mechanisms, e.g., in an old-fashioned computer using tubes and wires and in a more recent model using semiconductors and printed circuits. An object can instantiate an abstract automaton as long as it is capable of internal states and processes related as required by the program. It does not matter how it is constructed.

A detailed psychological model could be identified with an individual psychology. Anything that instantiates the associated automaton would have that individual psychology; and vice versa. Thus a person instantiates the automaton that serves as the model of his individual psychology. Given sufficient technology, a robot could be constructed that would also instantiate that individual psychology. From this point of view, the fact that the same psychological states and processes can be physically realized in different ways is an instance of the point that abstract automaton states and processes can be physically realized in different ways.

As Aristotle pointed out, mental states and processes are to be functionally defined. They are constituted by their function or role in the relevant program. To understand desire, belief, and reasoning is to understand how desires, beliefs, and instances of reasoning function in a human psychology.

A person's beliefs form his representation of the world, his desires represent his ends, goals, plans, and intentions. Perception yields new information about the world; natural needs for food, water, sleep, etc., put constraints on goals and intentions. Theoretical reasoning is a process that functions to improve his representation of the way things are. Practical reasoning is a way of modifying plans and intentions, in the light of the way things are represented to be, so as to increase the chances of success at reaching goals and ends. Pain functions to indicate danger or damage to parts of a person's body so as to get him out of a harmful situation or to care for the injury or to avoid such situations in the future. Certain emotions, such as fear, serve to concentrate his attention in a particular situation or some threat in the environment and enable him to avoid distractions.

These remarks are crude, but they bring out the way in which attention to the functional role of mental states and processes helps in explaining what they are.

6. Reasoning

Reasoning is a mental process. Since mental states and processes are functionally defined, to say what reasoning is is to say how it functions psychologically. To do that is to say how ascriptions of reasoning function in our accounts of people. Now it is in accordance with the strategy suggested at the conclusion of chapter one to suppose that the function of reasoning in giving a person knowledge is particularly relevant.

Chapter one suggested the use of intuitions about knowledge in the discovery of criteria of warranted inference and in determining when inference has occurred. This strategy will be pursued in detail below. It is important at this point to note a connection between the suggested strategy and a functionalist theory of mental states and processes.

Recall that Gettier was able to show that knowledge is not simply justified true belief. From premises one knows to be true one can inductively infer something false and be justified in doing so. One can go on to infer something true from that first conclusion and still be justified. One's second conclusion is true and one is justified in believing it; but one does not know that it is true. Therefore we are led to accept roughly the following principle:

P   Reasoning that essentially involves false conclusions, intermediate or final, cannot give one knowledge.

Many Gettier examples are not obviously accounted for by P, since it is not always evident that there has been any relevant reasoning. We can account for such cases by means of principle P if we *assume* that the relevant reasoning has occurred. As indicated in chapter one, it is not easy to decide directly whether reasoning has occurred in various examples. It is much easier to decide whether the examples are examples of knowledge and also whether the Gettier effect is operating. That is why I suggested that we use intuitions about knowledge and the Gettier effect to decide when reasoning has occurred and what reasoning there has been. What is presently of interest is that this is to treat reasoning as a functionally defined process that is partly specified in terms of its role in giving a person knowledge.

Thus we considered a man who comes to know something as the result of being told it by someone else. Even if what is said is true, the man does not come to know it if the speaker is not saying what he believes. Here is a Gettier example where there may be no obvious reasoning on the first man's part. However, if we ascribe reasoning to him we can account for our intuitions about knowledge. Roughly speaking, such reasoning would infer that the speaker says what he does because he believes it, he believes as he does because he has reason to believe it, and he has such reason because of the truth of what he believes. If the speaker did not believe what he says, the hearer's reasoning would infer something false; so, by principle P, his reasoning could not give him knowledge. Ascribing this reasoning to the hearer enables us to account for our intuitions about knowledge by means of a simple principle. A functional account of reasoning enables us to make sense of such ascription.

Words like "reasoning," "argument," and "inference" are ambiguous. They may refer to a process of reasoning, argument, or inference, or they may refer to an abstract structure consisting of certain propositions as premises, others as conclusions, perhaps others as intermediate steps. A functional account of reasoning says how a mental or neurophysiological process can *be* a process of reasoning by virtue of the way it functions. That is, a functional account says how the functioning of such a process allows it to be correlated with the reasoning, taken to be an abstract inference, which the process instantiates.

To be more precise, the relevant correlation is a mapping F from mental or neurophysiological processes to abstract structures of inference. If x is a process in the domain of F, then $F(x)$ is the (abstract) reasoning that x instantiates. Such a mapping F is a *reasoning instantiator*. To give a functional account of reasoning is to say which of the infinitely many possible mappings from processes to abstract inferences can serve as reasoning instantiators. For example, the conclusions arrived at

48

by reasoning must be beliefs reached by the process of reasoning. In other words, we are only interested in mappings F such that for any x in the domain of F there is a proposition h that is contained in the conclusion of $F(x)$ and x leads to belief in h (or would so lead if h were not already believed).

Furthermore, reasoning must be specified partly in terms of its role in giving a person knowledge. F must be such that whether process x can give knowledge depends, among other things, on the abstract reasoning $F(x)$. For example, x can lead one to be justified in believing h only if the reasons specifying $F(x)$ would warrant one in believing h. The extent to which possible knowledge of h depends on whether one knows other things that one believes must be reflected in the fact that these beliefs appear as premises, intermediate steps, or conclusions in $F(x)$. Finally, it must be possible to explicate Gettier examples by means of the relevant $F(x)$ and principle P.

Ordinary talk about reasons and reasoning is to be explicated by way of the notion of a reasoning instantiator. To ascribe reasoning r to someone is to presuppose the existence of a reasoning instantiator F and to claim that his belief resulted from a process x such that $F(x) = r$. I have already argued in chapter two, section 3 that explanation by reasons involves such ascription of reasoning. If both points are right, it follows that the ordinary concept of knowledge plays an important role in commonsense explanation by reasons.

Nothing in this account keeps it from being extended to cover cases in which one "directly" perceives that something is the case. Here too there are Gettier examples that can be accounted for if reasoning of the appropriate sort is ascribed to the perceiver (see chapter one, section 6). Recall the man who acquires the belief that there is a candle about twelve feet in front of him. Indeed there is; but a mirror intervenes between that candle and the man in question. What he sees is the reflection of a similar candle off to one side. He is justified in believing that there is a candle about twelve feet in front of him, and that belief is true. But he does not come to know that the candle is there. This Gettier example is accounted for if the reasoning instantiator ascribes to the man in question reasoning that infers that things look the way they do (or that the stimulation of his eye is as it is) because there is a candle twelve feet in front of him, etc. There is no requirement that the man be aware that things are looking a certain way to him, or aware that the stimulation of his eye has the relevant character. A good reasoning instantiator will ascribe such reasoning to him in this and similar cases. This simplifies the account of observational knowledge and unifies it with the rest of the theory of knowledge.

Here we might object that this is to extend the notion of reasoning far beyond anything permitted in ordinary usage. But that would be a mistake. Ordinary usage even permits us to ascribe calculation and reasoning to inanimate machines (computers); and ascription of inference and reasoning to the perceiver will come as no surprise to anyone familiar with the psychology of perception.[1]

---

[1] I return to this point in chapter eleven, section 2.

7. Nondeterministic explanation

When for purposes of psychological explanation we conceive of a person as an automaton, it is important that we do not conceive of him as a deterministic automaton. We do not believe that certain psychological states must be followed by others. Explaining why someone believes something is like explaining why a nondeterministic automaton is in a particular state. Various moves are possible at any moment. It is not assumed that it is determined which move he will make. It is assumed only that various moves are possible. We can explain how he got to wherever it was he got to without implying that he had to get there.

There may or may not be an underlying neurophysiological determinism. I do not know what to make of quantum physics, and the experts do not seem to agree. I am talking about psychological determinism. A physically determined device can instantiate a non-deterministic automaton. An explanation that refers to reasoning does not presuppose either an underlying determinism or an underlying indeterminism. It makes no presupposition either way.

It is helpful to think here of a simple probabilistic automaton, such as a roulette wheel. We assume that the wheel can take any of a number of states, all equally probable. The wheel instantiates a nondeterministic automaton. Perhaps, under some complex description, it also instantiates a deterministic automaton. Our explanations of various outcomes presuppose the nondeterministic way of looking at the wheel without committing us either way with respect to the deterministic viewpoint. Similarly, explanations of belief as the result of reasoning are nondeterministic without committing us either way with respect to an underlying determinism. Reasons may or may not be causes; but explanation by reasons is not causal or deterministic explanation. It describes the sequence of considerations that led to belief in a conclusion without supposing that the sequence was determined.

This is uncongenial to the "covering law" theory of explanation. But that theory has always seemed implausible when applied to ordinary psychological explanation. Philosophers have accepted it only because they did not like the apparent alternatives. Seeing a person as a nondeterministic automaton helps us to see why the covering-law theory breaks down in this case. The theory breaks down, not because psychological explanation appeals to a mysterious kind of sympathetic understanding, but because it is nondeterministic. When we consider the sort of explanation involved in saying why a purely nondeterministic automaton is in a particular state, we can see how psychological explanation can be a perfectly intelligible kind of explanation without being deterministic.

It has sometimes been suggested that the only sort of nondeterministic explanation is statistical explanation which shows an outcome to be probable given certain initial conditions. But (to anticipate briefly the discussion in chapter eight, section 4) competing explanations of a roulette wheel's coming up red fifty times in a row might be that (a) the wheel was fixed to do so and (b) the wheel was not fixed and this is one of those times when the improbable occurs. Alternative (b) offers a

nondeterministic explanation without showing the outcome to be probable on any initial conditions.

8. Summary

In this chapter we have been concerned with the nature of mental processes. After rejecting dualism, a
crude identity theory, and behaviorism, we adopted a
point of Ramsey's so as to yield a functional account of
mental states and processes. We were led to see a person as an automaton. To understand a type of mental
state or process is to see what function such states or
processes can have in a person's "program." For reasoning, an important function is its role in giving him
knowledge. And, since the relevant automaton is nondeterministic, explanation by reasons is nondeterministic.

The following chapters assume that the functionalist
account of mental states and processes is correct and try
to say something more about such states and processes,
in particular about their representational character and
about the relationship between thought and language.

Chapter 4

Thought and Meaning

In this chapter I will discuss the way in which the representational character of mental states is determined by function. I will speak of a "language of thought" and will speculate on the relations between the inner language of thought and the outer language we speak. In particular I will try to say how the meaning of the outer sentence can be in part a matter of the representational character of the inner sentence. This speculation prepares the ground for the theory, developed in the next two chapters, that we sometimes think in words. The suggestion forms the basis of an account of language and thought, which avoids analytic truths knowable simply by virtue of knowing their meaning, thus redeeming a promise from chapter one. The discussion of representation and structure in this and the next chapter also sets the stage for a later discussion of the relevance of deduction to inference in chapter ten.

1. Mental structure

The names of certain mental states are formed by combining the name of a type of state—belief, desire, hope, fear, or whatever—with a sentence. For example, we speak of "the belief that snow is white" or "the hope that war will end." This connection between states and sentences is no accident. Mental states can have structures that resemble the structures of the corresponding sentences, a fact we rely on in specifying logical and psychological relations among mental states.

Consider logical relations between beliefs. If the belief that *snow is white and grass is green* is true, the belief that *snow is white* is true; if the belief that *Harrisburg is the capital of Pennsylvania and Albany is the capital of New York* is true, the belief that *Harrisburg is the capital of Pennsylvania* is true; and so forth. Clearly, a generalization is possible: whenever the belief that $P \& Q$ is true, the corresponding belief that P is true. Some such general statement is appropriate. We cannot simply list the relevant instances, since there are an infinite number of them. But the relevant generalization presupposes that certain beliefs have the structure of conjunction.

Corresponding to the belief that P and the belief that Q is the conjunctive belief that $P \& Q$, which is true if and only if both of the former beliefs—its conjuncts—are true. Furthermore, there is the disjunctive belief that $P \lor Q$, which is true if and only if either of the former beliefs—this time its disjuncts—are true; and there is the negative belief that $\sim P$, which is true if and only if the belief that P is not true. There are also conjunctive, disjunctive, and negative desires, hopes, and fears: for example, the conjunctive hope that $P \& Q$ will *come* true just in case its conjuncts—the hope that P and the hope that Q—come true. Mental states have structure, and logical relations hold among those states by virtue of that structure.

55

Explanations by reasons typically presuppose this mental structure. For example, we sometimes cite the desire that P and the belief that Q *if* P in order to explain the desire that Q. That sort of explanation assumes belief can have the conditional structure, Q *if* P. Furthermore, it is evident that explanations of beliefs often mention other beliefs logically related to the beliefs explained. Since logical relations among mental states depend on the structure of those states, these explanations also appeal to structure.

We will see that the syntactic structure of a sentence represents the way the sentence is constructed out of names, predicates, logical connectives, variables, quantifiers, and so forth (see chapter five, section 1). The infinity of possible sentences is constructible out of finite resources because those resources can be put together in different ways. The structure of a mental state similarly represents the way it can be constructed from mental names, mental predicates, mental connectives, mental variables, mental quantifiers, and so forth. For example, the belief that $P\&Q$ can be constructed from the belief that P and the belief that Q by an operation of conjunction; and analogously for other complex states. Finite resources give rise to a potential infinity of mental states.

2. *The language of thought*

Not only do mental states have structure in something like the way in which corresponding sentences have structure, they also have representational characteristics in something like the way that sentences do. And, as in the case of sentences, representational characteristics of mental states depend on structure. Just as we can talk about Paul Benacerraf, we can have beliefs about him, as well as fears, hopes, desires, and so forth. Just as our remarks can represent Benacerraf as wise, so can our beliefs, fears, hopes, and desires. And just as what we say can be true, beliefs can be true and fears, hopes, and desires can come true. The belief that Benacerraf is wise, the hope that he is wise, the fear that he is wise, and the desire that he be wise are all about Benacerraf, and all represent him as wise. The difference between these mental states is a matter of the difference in the attitude they represent toward Benacerraf's being wise. They are true, or come true, if Benacerraf turns out to be wise.

Let us speak as if there were a "language of thought" and that mental states essentially involve "sentences" of this language. Then, to believe that Benacerraf is wise is to be in a relationship to a sentence of the language of thought, and to desire that Benacerraf be wise is to be in a different relationship to the same sentence. Representational characteristics of mental states derive from representational characteristics of sentences of the language of thought. For example, to come to believe that Benacerraf is wise is to form an instance of the appropriate sentence and store it among our set of beliefs. To come to want Benacerraf to be wise is to form another instance of the same sentence and store it among our ends; and similarly for other mental states. We can envision a psychological model in which believed sentences are actually stored in one place and desired sentences are stored in another; but we do not have to assume that beliefs and desires have distinct locations in the human brain, so long as there is some difference between an instance of a sentence of the language of thought stored as a belief and an instance of that sentence stored as an end.

This suggestion that there is a language of thought is easy to verify. We can simply take mental states to *be* instances or "tokens" of appropriate sentences. The belief that Benacerraf is wise will then be the appropriate sentence of the language of thought stored as a belief; and the desire that Benacerraf be wise will be the same sentence stored as an end. We can take these states to be instances of sentences because they have structure and representational characteristics that depend on their structure. In the same way, instances of sentences of a language used in communication are utterances and inscriptions. Just as various speech acts—promises, threats, warnings, and so forth—can involve instances of the same sentence of the outer language, various mental states—beliefs, desires, hopes, and so forth—can be instances of the same sentence of the inner language of thought.

This is to agree with philosophers who say that thoughts involve the use of symbols, but not for the reasons that have often been suggested. Ayer writes, ". . . I want to insist that if the thought is to be a thought *of* something or a thought *that* such and such is so, it must be expressed in symbols of some sort. This is, indeed, analytic: unless it were so expressed I should not allow that it was a thought of anything or a thought that anything was so" (p. 29). Ayer's view is that if the putative thought does not involve symbolic expression, we should refuse to call it a thought. My point is the converse: if it is a thought we can call it a symbol. Since thoughts have representational characteristics that depend on their structure, they are trivially part of a symbolic system. It is trivial that a thought involves symbolic expression because the thought can trivially be identified with a symbolic expression, namely an instance of a sentence in what I am calling the language of thought.

Of course, there are important differences between the use of language in communication and what I shall call its use in thought. The statement that Benacerraf is wise refers to Benacerraf, means that he is wise, and may or may not be understood by someone. None of these things is true of the belief that Benacerraf is wise, if "refer," "mean," and "understand" are used strictly in their ordinary senses. Although such a belief is about Benacerraf and represents him as wise, it does not in any ordinary sense *refer* to him, it does not *mean* that he is wise, and it is not *understood* or misunderstood by anyone. Nor, in simply having such a belief, do we in any ordinary sense *refer* to Benacerraf or *mean* that he is wise. Reference, meaning, and understanding, as we ordinarily understand these things, have to do with the use of language in communication and not with its use in thought.

3. Meaning

A functional account of mental states and processes is an account of the language of thought, since mental states are instances of sentences of the language of thought. The representational character of a sentence of that inner language depends on its potential role—the role of possible instances of the sentence—in the functional system. No wonder some philosophers have suggested that the *meaning* of a sentence is its role in the system or, as is sometimes said, its role in a conceptual scheme.

A complication arises from the fact that only sentences of the inner language of thought have roles in a functional system, whereas only sentences of the outer language used in communication have meaning, in any ordinary sense of "meaning." So we must say that what a sentence used in communication means depends in part on the role of a corresponding sentence in the language of thought. Outer language is used to express beliefs and other mental states. To specify the meaning of a sentence used in communication is partly to specify the belief or other mental state expressed; and the representational character of that state is determined by its functional role. Since the state expressed is an instance of a sentence of the inner language of thought, the meaning of an outer sentence is at least partly a matter of the role in thought of the inner sentence it expresses.

It is in accord with ordinary usage to reserve the title "theory of meaning" for a theory of communication that explains the relation between an utterance and the mental states it expresses. A functional account of mental states can be called an account of representational character. Theories of meaning in the strict sense range from crude causal views, according to which meaning is a matter of the state which tends to cause an utterance and which the utterance tends to cause in the audience, to Grice's sophisticated theory that meaning is a matter of the state the speaker intends his audience to think he is in by virtue of their recognition of his intention.

A theory of truth in a language is often somewhat misleadingly called a theory of meaning (or a "semantics") for the language. A theory of truth shows how truth conditions of a sentence depend on its structure, and is only indirectly related to a theory of meaning strictly so called, since it is part of a theory that shows how representational characteristics depend on structure. I will come back to this point in the next chapter.

Finally, the name "theory of meaning" is sometimes given to a general theory of speech acts, which includes a theory of communication but also tries to account for the differences among promises, threats, warnings, requests, and so forth. However, since it is not clear that the difference between a threat and a promise need make a difference to the meaning of what is said (although presumably it represents a difference in what the speaker means to be doing), I will reserve the title "theory of meaning" for the theory of communication.

In summary, four different sorts of theory have been at one time or another called theories of meaning: the theory of representational character, the theory of communication, the theory of truth, and the theory of speech acts. These theories do not compete with each other. The theory of truth is part of the theory of representational character, which is presupposed by the theory of communication, which in turn is contained in the more general theory of speech acts. Of these theories, the theory of communication is most appropriately called the theory of meaning, although each of the theories is relevant to meaning in one way or another.

4. Role and representation

The best way to see how functional role affects representational character is to begin with simple examples and gradually make them more complicated. We should assume at first that circumstances are normal and that no mistakes are made. Then mistakes can be understood as abnormalities.

In elementary cases, a belief state that represents a particular thing normally results from the perception of that thing and leads to behavior involving that thing. What the thing is represented *as* depends on this behavior. For example, an animal perceives something as food if it treats it as food, e.g., if it eats it. It has a belief state representing the food as food, because it has a state resulting from the perception of the food which leads to its eating that food.[1]

Belief that something is food may or may not lead to the attempt to eat it. Another state must be present if this is to happen: hunger, or the desire to eat. That this state is hunger derives from the way it is connected with perception of food, the need for food, and eating. A resulting state, the desire to eat a particular thing, gains its representational character from the states that give rise to it as well as the action which it perhaps directly produces.

[1] Dennett, p. 73.

Things can go wrong with this simple picture. The desire to eat may be overshadowed by other desires, so no eating occurs. We can still attribute this desire to the animal because it is in a state that would normally, or other things being equal, or sometimes, lead to eating. Or the overeager animal can think that it sees food where there is none. Again we attribute a psychological state by referring to the normal case. The animal is in a state normally caused by the presence of food and normally leading to eating.

Something like a background of normality figures in all identifications of representational states. A device that takes data from radar and fires guns to shoot down planes represents the planes as at a particular location and as going to be at a different location. That description is appropriate because radar waves from the planes influence what we call the representation of the planes; and that representation plays a role in firing the guns that shoot them down. We can say this even though the guns miss as the result of a sudden change of course or even though a flock of birds sets off the cycle. We can say it because we have a conception of the normal operation of the device. That enables us to retain this way of talking about the device even when it is disconnected from radar and guns for a test in the laboratory. On the other hand, if our conception of normal working is different, the device must be described differently. If the planes are not likely to be what is responsible for the radar signals—and if the response is not correct for shooting down planes—and if nothing has gone wrong with the machine—then we would not suppose that it represents where planes have been and are going to be.

These remarks must be ramified and extended. Other sorts of activity besides eating and shooting are relevant to the representation of something as other than food or an enemy. For example, representing something as an obstacle might lead to going around it. But most concepts will not be associated with simple activities. That makes it difficult to say what it is for a psychological state to represent something as something, since it is not enough that the state result from observation of the relevant thing. It must also make possible appropriate action with respect to that thing; and we cannot easily say what appropriate action would be.

Furthermore, representations often have an evidential function. Food in a particular location may be the sign of a nearby predator. In that case, the representation of something as food may function to produce the representation of danger. Almost any belief can function in inference concerned with a variety of subjects; and some representations seem to function only as signs —representations of color, for example. The representation of something as red can function evidentially in various ways in various contexts; but there is no activity appropriate to the representation of something as red in the way that eating is appropriate to the representation of something as food. In this case, the possible evidential function is enough. The representation of something as red makes appropriate action possible with respect to that thing, since inference can connect a representation of something as red with its representation, e.g., as food.

Observe that this account of representation implies that a system of mental representation must represent an objective public world and not just subjective private experience. A mental representation has the character it has not only by virtue of direct or indirect connection with observation, but also by virtue of a connection with activities that satisfy needs of the organism and/or by virtue of connections with other representations more directly tied to such activities. Some representations must concern the satisfaction of needs of the organism by means of appropriate behavior; those representations involve representation of a public world. The needs of the organism are facts about its *body*. Therefore, what is represented cannot be just the subjective phenomenon of behavior but must be actual behavior that would actually satisfy the bodily needs in question.[2]

5. *Summary*

Mental states have structure in the way that sentences have structure; in both cases representational characteristics of the whole depend on this structure. Mental states are part of a system of representation that can be called a language of thought. The theory that meaning is a matter of role in a conceptual scheme is in the first instance best treated as a theory not of meaning but of the representational character of sentences of the language of thought, which is to say of the mental states that instantiate those sentences. So understood, the theory amounts to a functionalist theory of mental states.

Chapter five examines the theory of truth taken as an

[2] Another complication is that representational character can depend on the social history of a term, what Kaplan calls genetic factors. See also Donnellan; and especially Kripke.

account of the way representational characteristics depend on structure, and it examines connections between the sort of structure required by the theory of truth and that required by grammar. Chapter six makes use of the results of chapter five to consider again the connections between inner and outer languages, between thought and communication. Finally, later chapters make an extended investigation into the nature of inference as it bears on role in conceptual scheme.

Chapter 5

Truth and Structure

An account of the nature of thought must attempt to explain the relationship between thought and language, how thought is expressed in language, and how language molds thought. In chapter six I will argue that language provides not only a vehicle of communication but equally importantly a medium of thought, for I will suggest that in learning language we learn to think in words. But thoughts cannot be construed as simply strings of words; they must be taken to have the structure of sentences under analysis. That is why in the present chapter I will try to say something about the syntactic and truth-conditional analysis of sentences. The truth-conditional structures I talk about are the structures of the thoughts that the sentences express. Syntactic analysis is relevant since, I will be claiming, thoughts are sometimes sentences analyzed into truth-conditional structures.

1. Truth conditions

The representational character of a sentence in a language like English depends not only on the words in the sentence but also on the way the sentence is constructed out of those words. The same words can be put together in different ways to yield sentences with different meanings. *John hit Bob* is not synonymous with *Bob hit John* since, although the two sentences contain the same words, they are not constructed in the same way out of those words.

The construction of a sentence is not simply a matter of the order of the words in the sentence. Consider syntactical ambiguity. (1) *They are visiting doctors* can mean either (2) *they are visiting some doctors* or (3) *they are doctors who are visiting*. The structure of (1) can resemble the structure of (2) or that of (3). Either way to construct (1) yields the same words in the same order; but the representational character of (1) varies depending how it is thought to be constructed.

The truth conditions of a sentence provide a clue to its construction. A sentence of the form *A hit B* is true if and only if what *A* designates hit what *B* designates. *Hit* is a "predicate" with two "arguments," *A* and *B*; and the difference between *John hit Bob* and *Bob hit John* is a matter of which arguments the names are. The first sentence is constructed by applying the predicate *hit* to the arguments *John* and *Bob* in that order. The second is constructed by applying the same predicate to the same arguments in the reverse order. So, the structures can be represented respectively as *hit (John, Bob)* and *hit (Bob, John)*.

They are visiting doctors has different truth conditions depending on how it is interpreted. A sentence of the form *A are B* is true if and only if the things designated by *A* are among the things designated by *B*. On the other hand, a sentence of the form *A are visiting B* is true if and only if the things designated by *A* are visiting the things designated by *B*. *They are visiting doctors* is ambiguous because it can have either of two structures. It can be constructed by applying the predicate *are* to the arguments *they* and *visiting doctors*; and it can also be constructed by applying the predicate *are visiting* to the arguments *they* and *doctors*. It can have either the structure *are (they, visiting-doctors)* or the structure *are-visiting (they, doctors)*.

So far as truth conditions are concerned, the relevant structure need not be right on the surface. *B was hit by A* has the same truth conditions as *A hit B*. In either case the predicate *hit* is applied to the arguments *A* and *B* in that order; the relevant structure is *hit (A, B)* in both cases. Which expression turns up as subject in the spoken sentence is not so important. *John hit Bob* and *John was hit by Bob* have the same "subject" and the same "object" but have different structures, where the difference in structure is a matter of the order of the arguments to which the predicate *hit* is applied.

Furthermore, sentences with similar surface form can have quite different truth-conditional structures. The following sentences have similar surface forms: *John hit Bob, somebody hit Bob*, and *nobody hit Bob*. The relevant differences in truth-conditional structures of these sentences can be brought out by considering implications among them. *John hit Bob* implies *somebody hit Bob*, but *nobody hit Bob* does not. *Nobody hit Bob* has a relevantly different structure from that of the other sentences. Its structure might be represented as *not (somebody hit Bob)*. It is constructed by negating the sentence *somebody hit Bob*, i.e., by applying *not* to the latter sentence. The connection with truth conditions is that the negation of a sentence is true if and only if the sentence is not true. *Nobody hit Bob* is to be analyzed as containing *somebody hit Bob* and as denying it.

Somebody hit Bob itself has a different structure from that of *John hit Bob*. When *John hit Bob* is used, *John* is taken to designate a particular person. *John hit Bob* is true if and only if the person designated by *John* hit the person designated by *Bob*. However, when *somebody hit Bob* is used, *somebody* is not necessarily taken to designate a particular person. Even if the speaker has a particular person in mind, we cannot suppose that *somebody hit Bob* is true if and only if that person hit the person designated by *Bob*. If the person the speaker has in mind did not hit Bob but some other person did, *somebody hit Bob* is still true. The same point emerges if we consider possible implications. Both *John hit Bob* and *George hit Bob* imply *somebody hit Bob*; but not vice versa. So *somebody* is not just another name like *John* or *George*.

Somebody represents an "existential quantifier." The structure of *somebody hit Bob* might be represented as $(\Sigma x) (hit(x, Bob))$, read *for some x, x hit Bob*. The existential quantifier (Σx) is a sentential operator. It has been applied here to $hit(x, Bob)$, which is called an "open sentence" because it contains the "free variable" x. $(\Sigma x) (hit(x, Bob))$ is a "closed sentence" because x has been "bound" by the existential quantifier. A sentence of the form $(\Sigma x)(S)$ is true if and only if, for some a, S

70

is true when x is taken to designate a. The sentence *John hit everyone* involves universal quantification. Its structure is $(x)(hit(John, x))$, read "for every x, John hit x." A sentence of the form (x) (S) is true if and only if S comes out true no matter what x is taken to designate. Quantifiers can be combined. *Somebody hit everyone* has the structure (Σx) (y) $(hit(x,y))$; and *everyone hit somebody* has the structure (x) (Σy) $(hit(x, y))$. These are not the only possible interpretations of those sentences. Many people can hear *somebody hit everyone* as having the structure (y) (Σx) $(hit(x, y))$; and many can hear *everyone hit somebody* as (Σy) (x) $(hit(x, y))$.

A theory of truth for a language shows how the truth conditions of any sentence depend on the structure of that sentence. The theory will say, for each element of structure, what its contribution is. The theory will imply an infinite set of statements of the form *x is true if and only if s*, where x is replaced by a name of a sentence Φ that enables one to determine Φ's structure and s is replaced by the sentence Φ itself or a sentence that is true if and only if Φ is. Each such instance gives the truth conditions of a sentence of the language. For example, consider *somebody hit everyone* with the structure (Σx) (y) $(hit(x, y))$. The clause for existential quantification tells us that this sentence is true if and only if, for some a, (y) $(hit(x, y))$ is true when x designates a. The clause for universal quantification tells us that (y) $(hit(x, y))$ is true if and only if $hit(x, y)$ is true no matter what y designates. So we learn that (Σx) (y) $(hit(x, y))$ is true if and only if, for some a and for every b, where x designates a and y designates b,

71

hit(x, y) is true. But *hit(x, y)* is true if and only if what *x* designates hit what *y* designates. So $(\Sigma x)\,(y)\,(hit(x,y))$ is true if and only if, for some *a* and for every *b*, where *x* designates *a* and *y* designates *b*, what *x* designates hit what *y* designates. In other words, it is true if and only if, for some *a* and for every *b*, *a* hit *b*. It is true if and only if somebody hit everyone.

In general, sentences of a natural language are not true or false by themselves, even given a fixed understanding of their structure. *I hit him* is true in one mouth, false in another; true at one time, false at another; true of one person designated as *him*, false of another. Even *John hit Bob* can be true of one *John* and *Bob* but false of another pair. Sentences are true or false relative to a speaker, an audience, a time, a place, assignments of designations to pronouns, names, and other designating phrases, etc. We can abbreviate this by saying that sentences are true or false relative to an assignment. When I said above that the theory of truth will imply statements of the form *x is true if and only if s*, it would have been more accurate to say that it will imply statements of the form *for any assignment q, x is true relative to q if and only if s*, where *x* is replaced by a structural descriptive name of a sentence Φ and *s* is replaced by a sentence like Φ (or a sentence true if and only if Φ is true) except that references to speaker, audience, time, etc. are replaced by "what *q* assigns as the speaker," "what *q* assigns as audience," etc.

The theory will imply statements of that form for every sentence of the language that does not contain "semantic terms" like *true*. We cannot insist that the theory imply such statements for all sentences, even those containing *true* if we want to avoid paradox. There will always be statements like this:

(*) (*) is not true.

But, if the theory of truth implies the corresponding instance of *x is true if and only if s*, it will imply that (*) is true if and only if (*) is not true, which is an inconsistent remark. And if a theory implies something that is inconsistent, the theory cannot be true. So we will not want the theory to imply instances like that.

The problem posed by sentences like (*) is that if we arc not careful they lead to contradictions, the so-called semantic paradoxes. I will not say here what I think is the best way to avoid such paradoxes in the theory of truth.

2. *Grammar and logical form*

An adequate theory of truth for a language provides us with a grammar of the language. A grammar is a set of rules for constructing sentences out of their parts. It can be divided into two sets of rules, rules for constructing truth-conditional structures like $(\Sigma x) (y) (hit(x, y))$, and rules for transforming those structures into the surface forms of sentences like *somebody hit everyone*. For the present I will be talking about the first part of the grammar. In the next section I will discuss the transformational rules.

Certain grammatical rules are immediately derivable from clauses in the theory of truth. For example, a (truth-conditional) structure can be formed by applying the predicate *hit* to two arguments. Arguments can be names or variables. A structure can also be formed by applying negation to a structure, or by applying conjunction or disjunction to two structures, or by applying existential or universal quantification to a structure with the relevant free variable.

These rules can be simplified and systematized if we group structural elements into grammatical categories: predicates, arguments, connectives (*not, and, or*), and quantifiers. A structure can be formed by applying a predicate to the appropriate number of arguments, by applying a connective to the appropriate number of structures, or by applying a quantifier to a structure with the appropriate free variable.

Notice that some grammatical categories have indefinitely many members, e.g., predicates and arguments. Other categories have only a few members, e.g., connectives and quantifiers. The members of the latter categories are *logical elements* of structure. A structure represents a *logical truth* if there is no uniform way to substitute for nonlogical elements that makes the structure represent something false.[1] For example, in the structure of *John hit Bob or John did not hit Bob*, i.e., *(hit(John, Bob)) or (not(hit(John, Bob)))*, the nonlogical elements are *hit, John*, and *Bob*. The sentence is a logical truth, since there is no way to substitute in its structure uniformly for *hit, John*, and *Bob* in order to make it false; for example, it is also true that *(killed(Caesar, Brutus)) or (not(killed(Caesar, Brutus)))*, i.e., it is true either that Caesar killed Brutus or that Caesar did not kill Brutus. But even if John hit Bob, the sentence *John*

[1] Quine.

hit Bob, with the structure *hit(John, Bob)*, is not a logical truth, since there is a way to substitute for nonlogical elements in its structure to get the structure of something false, since *killed(Caesar, Brutus)* is the structure of *Caesar killed Brutus*, which is false.

One sentence logically implies a second if there is no way to substitute uniformly for the nonlogical elements throughout the structures of both sentences in order to make the first sentence true and the second false. For example, *hit(John, Bob)* or *John hit Bob* logically implies *(Σx) (hit(x, Bob))* or *someone hit Bob*. No uniform substitution for nonlogical structural elements makes the first of these sentences true, the second false. Notice that *s* logically implies *t* if and only if *(not s) or t* is a logical truth.

The logical form of a sentence is that part of its structure that involves logical elements. So a logical truth is a sentence such that no sentence with the same logical form is false; and a logical implication is one that holds by virtue of logical form in the sense that, for any pair of sentences of that form, if the first is true, the second is also true.

Therefore, a theory of logical form can be associated with a grammar and theory of truth. The theory of logical form assigns logical forms to sentences, and states rules of logical implication. Given the theory, we should be able to show that all instances of these rules are in fact logical implications and that the rules account for all logical implications. Furthermore, the theory of logical form must account for all implications that speakers take to be obvious by means of a finite set of axioms or obvious truths. The obvious implications should turn out to be either logical implications themselves, or convertible into logical implications by conjoining one or more axioms to the first sentence of the implication.

If all obvious implications could not be accounted for by means of a finite list of axioms, something would be wrong with the theory of logical form. To make use of an infinite number of axioms, i.e., an axiom schema, would be in effect to introduce an additional rule of logic. Any such rule must be justified by appeal to logical form, as already indicated. So, logical forms assigned to sentences would have to be modified; and that would require a change in grammar and perhaps even in the theory of truth.

I have been speaking as if there were a single correct theory of truth for a language, a single grammar, and a single theory of logical form. But quite different theories are possible; and different theories of logical form yield different suggestions as to what the logical implications are. Obvious implications that one theory accounts for by means of axioms and rules of logic, a different theory accounts for by means of logic alone; this situation will be reversed with respect to other obvious implications. This large number of possible theories can be somewhat diminished and brought under some control if we try to keep the rules of logic as close as possible to those of ordinary (first-order) quantification theory (with identity) and attempt to minimize axioms and any ontological commitment ascribed to sentences whose logical form is given.

Some sort of theory of logical form is involved in any theory of truth for a natural language and, more generally, in any account of representational character. It is involved in the theory of truth since, e.g., there is no way to show that the theory implies *"snow is white* is true if and only if snow is white" unless an assumption is made about the logical form of "snow is white" on the right-hand side of this equivalence. The more general point is that representational character has to do with role in conceptual scheme, and role in conceptual scheme has something to do with logical implication, so that any adequate theory of representational character must make use of a theory of logical form.

3. *Transformations and ambiguity*

Rules of grammar include not only rules for the building of truth-conditional structures but also rules that can be used to transform those structures into the surface forms of sentences. I mention here some transformational rules a grammar might state, with examples of their effects.

Subject formation would convert *hit(x, y)* into *x(hit y)*. *Not* placement would convert *not(x(hit y))* into *x(did not(hit y))*. Quantifier placement would convert *(Σx)(y)(x(hit y))* first into *(Σx)(x(hit everyone))* and then into *someone(hit everyone)*. Passive would convert *hit (x, y)* into *was hit (y(by x))*, which subject formation would convert into *y(was hit(by x))*.

(I have oversimplified and have ignored complications. The nature of the relevant transformations is studied in the theory of the transformational grammar, which is a complex subject involving many controversial points. Many of these complexities and controversies—but not all—must be ignored here if we are not to go off on a tangent.)

When structures with different truth conditions can be grammatically transformed into the same surface form, the resulting sentence is ambiguous. *They are visiting doctors* is ambiguous because it can be derived either from *are(they, visiting doctors)* or from *are visiting(they, doctors)*. *Someone hit everyone* is ambiguous because it can come from $(\Sigma x)(y)(hit(x, y))$ or from $(y)(\Sigma x)(hit(x, y))$.

A different type of ambiguity derives from the ambiguity of a word. *John is near a bank* is ambiguous because *bank* is ambiguous. The underlying truth-conditional structures of its two interpretations look the same, e.g., $(\Sigma x)(bank(x)\ \&\ near(John, x))$. The truth conditions of these structures differ because of a difference in the conditions under which something is a bank in one or the other sense. Now, a good way to indicate the ambiguity of the word *bank* is to suppose that there are two underlying predicates, *bank$_1$* and *bank$_2$*, with different truth conditions. Then the underlying structures of *John is near a bank* can be distinguished: $(\Sigma x)(bank_1(x)\ \&\ near(John, x))$ versus $(\Sigma x)(bank_2(x)\ \&\ near(John, x))$. So it is possible to assimilate the second type of ambiguity to the first. Any ambiguity can be taken to be a kind of grammatical ambiguity in the sense that it can be taken to result from the possibility of transforming different underlying truth-conditional structures into the same surface form.

4. Truth-conditional structure as language dependent

Although truth-conditional structures in different languages may have many things in common, there is no reason to suppose that exactly the same structures underlie surface forms of sentences in different languages. Truth-conditional structures can be specific to a language in the sense that basic predicates that appear in truth-conditional structure are not the same from one language to another.

It is sometimes suggested that the same basic structures occur in all languages and that the difference between two languages is a difference in the transformational rules that map basic structures into surface forms. This suggestion fits in well with the idea that truth-conditional structures are sentences in what I am calling the language of thought, if we also suppose that differences between natural languages are differences in the ways that sentences are correlated with thoughts.

Now in chapter six I will argue that sentences of the language of thought do include truth-conditional structures of a natural language; but I will also argue that these structures, and hence the relevant thoughts, are language-dependent. What we can think depends in part on the language we speak.

It is sometimes suggested that, on the contrary, basic predicates in one language are transformationally derived from more basic predicates common to all languages. For example, it has been argued that *kill* is transformationally derived from *(cause) to (become) (not) (alive)*, where *(cause)*, *(become)*, *(not)*, and *(alive)* are not the corresponding English words but are predicates that appear in the underlying structures of sentences in all languages. The argument for this is that some such analysis is needed in order to account for the differences between *I slowly killed him*, in the sense that I slowly did something that caused his death, and *I killed him slowly* in the sense that I did something that caused him to die slowly. If *kill* appears as an unanalyzed notion in the truth-conditional structure of *I killed him*, then there is only one thing represented in that structure which can be said to be slow—my killing of the person in question. So it would seem that only one of the interpretations in question can be represented. On the other hand, if *I killed him* is taken to have a structure like that of *I did something that caused him to become not alive*, at least two different things can be represented as slow, what I did—the killing—and his becoming not alive—the dying. Only if *kill* is given some analysis in underlying structure will we be able to represent both interpretations.

But this is a weak argument. At best it shows that *kill* derives from *cause to die*. It offers no reason at all to derive *die* from *become not alive*. And it provides no reason to suppose that the underlying predicates in these structures are predicates all languages have in common rather than predicates specific to English.[2]

---

[2] Other arguments have also been given; but none is as convincing as the argument concerning *kill*. Postal claims that linguistic facts about one sense of the word *remind* can be accounted for only if the underlying structure of *x reminds y of z* is something like that underlying *y perceives that x is similar to z*; Lakoff claims that *dissuade* must be derived from *persuade . . . not*. However, these arguments are in both cases quite weak. For example, Postal's argument seems to confuse a way in which something can remind us of something else with a sense of the word *remind*. Lakoff argues that the behavior of quantifiers and negation with respect to *dissuade* can be accounted for in terms of two principles he advocates only if *x dissuades y from*

It is probably true that basic concepts like negation, causality, becoming, quantification, life, etc., can be expressed in all languages. But it also seems true that there are many predicates of any given language that resist translation into another language, and that is hard to understand if all predicates are supposed to be transformationally derived from a stock of basic predicates that all languages have in common. To take a very simple example, languages that divide the color cone differently have words for colors that are not intertranslatable. Surely there is no underlying stock of color predicates common to all languages in terms of which the color predicates of particular languages are to be analyzed. And any predicates that, like color predicates, are learned by examining examples of things that satisfy them would seem to be also like color predicates in not being definable by means of predicates common to the underlying structures of all languages. So it is highly unlikely that there is a basic set of underlying structures common to all languages. The difference between two languages is not just a difference in transformations that map basic structures onto surface structures.

Many linguists have supposed that an adequate gram-

---

z is derived from something like the structure underlying x *persuades* y *not to* z; but his data can be accounted for without that last assumption if we suppose instead that only one of the two principles he states applies to *dissuade*.

Again, even if these arguments concerning *remind* and *dissuade* were to be accepted, they would not by themselves show that the predicates from which these words are derived are common to underlying structures of all languages rather than being predicates specific to English.

mar must state principles that relate a sentence and its possible meanings, where sentences in different languages can have the same meanings. It might be suggested that, when this task is taken into consideration, the best grammar of a language will transformationally derive the surface forms of sentences from language-independent "semantic representations." But there exists no evidence that a grammar that associates sentences with semantic representations is simplified by transformationally deriving the sentence from a language-independent semantic representation. Furthermore, as I shall argue in chapter six, there are excellent reasons to doubt the existence of language-independent meanings. So there are good reasons to believe that grammar should not attempt to associate such meanings with sentences. Truth-conditional structures underlying the sentences of a language are specific to that language.

5. Summary

The representational character of a sentence, be it a sentence of the language used in communication or a sentence of the inner language of thought—i.e., a mental state—depends on its truth-conditional structure. What the sentence or state is about, what it represents, depends on what is designated by arguments in that structure. What the sentence or state represents something *as* depends on the predicates applied to the relevant arguments. The theory of truth thus shows how the representational character of a sentence or state is a function of the way it is constructed.

The theory of this structure, that is, the grammar, and the theory of truth together yield a theory of logical form that must account for obvious implications. Representational character is a matter of logical form inasmuch as it depends on role in conceptual scheme, because role in conceptual scheme depends in part on logical implications that hold between sentences or states.

The surface forms of sentences of a natural language are not the same as their truth-conditional structures. Grammatical transformations map the underlying structures onto the relevant surface forms. Ambiguity results when two different truth-conditional structures get transformed into the same surface sentence. The underlying truth-conditional structures are unambiguous. Perhaps the truth-conditional structures of sentences in a natural language are the same as the structures of the thoughts those sentences express. If so, the relevant thoughts are language-dependent, since the truth-conditional structures of sentences of natural languages are language-dependent.

Chapter 6

Thought and Language

1. Thinking in words

Language makes thought possible. Learning a language is not just learning a new way to put our thoughts into words; it is also learning a new way to think. In learning our first language we acquire a vast array of conceptual resources we did not have before. And learning a second language is not just learning to translate between it and the first language. We have not fully learned a language until we can think in it so that such translation is no longer necessary.

Not all mental states involve the language we speak; not all thought is in words. Animals often solve complex problems, and it would be arbitrary to deny that they can think. Babies have thoughts, beliefs, and desires before they learn a language. And many instances of adult thinking seem independent of language. Consider a chess-player trying to frame a strategy, a mechanic trying to decide what is wrong with the motor of a car, or an artist thinking whether to apply a dab of paint at a particular spot on the canvas. It would be totally inappropriate to suggest that the thinking involved in these cases *must* be in words. All this is compatible with what I am saying, which is not that all thoughts and mental states are in language but rather that some are. To say that language-learning is the acquisition of a new mode of thought is not to say there is no other mode of thought.

Ordinary linguistic communication seems to make use of the ability to think out loud. We do not usually first form a thought and then put it into words; nor does an audience normally first hear what we say and then decode it into a nonlinguistic thought. In order to understand what has been said it is normally enough to hear it as the appropriate sentence under the appropriate analysis, i.e., as the appropriate surface structure form correlated with the appropriate underlying truth-conditional structure. Of course, the chess-player, mechanic, and artist can tell us what they are thinking; so there is a sense in which they can express in words thoughts that were not originally in words. But in a more basic sense, the thoughts they would express occur in the words used to express them, since they express present thoughts about earlier thoughts. Their present thoughts are thoughts in language about thoughts that were not in language.

The chess-player, mechanic, and artist are not good examples of normal linguistic communication. Normally, we do not first have a thought and then express it in words. We simply think out loud. It is true that sometimes we cannot get a word in edgewise, and at such times a thought occurs before we have a chance to say it; but at such times the thought occurs as something to say in words.

Occasionally we have difficulty in expressing a thought. It takes some time to find the right words. Here there may seem to be a clear case of a thought that must be distinguished from the words used to communicate it. But we can grope for the right words even when the original thought is in words, if the uttering of those words would, for one or another reason, be inappropriate. We search for another way to "say the same thing." That is, we search for a form of words in certain respects equivalent to (but in other respects different from) the words that originally occurred to us. Similarly, we may search for a verbal thought that is in certain respects equivalent to a nonverbal thought. When we are successful, the thought communicated is thought in the words said aloud; and that thought is in certain respects equivalent to (but in other respects different from) our original thought.

Ryle objects to this sort of talk. "I want," he says, "to deny that it even makes sense to ask, in the general case, what special sort or sorts of things we think *in*." He agrees that "an Englishman who has become perfectly familiar with the French language may say that he can now think in French." But this is a "very special case."

> The primary thing that he means when he says that he now thinks in French is that when he has to talk to Frenchmen, he does not any longer have to think out how to say in French what he wants to say. He no longer, for example, has first to say to himself in English what he wants to say, and then to struggle to translate from English into French for the benefit of his French audience. The composition of French remarks is no longer any more difficult for him than the composition of English remarks, that is, it is not

difficult at all. But to say that he no longer has to think out how to say things in French has not the slightest tendency to show that all or most of the thoughts that he thinks are accompanied or "carried" by the production of French words. It is only to say that *when he is conversing with Frenchmen* he does not have to think about the vehicles of this conversing (p. 13).

Ryle agrees that some thinking involves words, e.g., thinking about what to say in a poem. He also notes the role of language and other symbolic systems in calculations of any complexity. Thus, he says,

> Trying to get the correct answer, unlike just making a guess at it, involves trying to establish checkable intermediate steps, in order to make the correct moves from these steps to the right answer; and these, to be checkable, must be formulated. . . . Some kinds of problems like those of advocates, debaters, and philosophers, have something in common with the task of composition and something in common with the task of computation. The thinker has, all the time, both to be trying to find out what to say and how to say it, and also to be trying to establish as true what he says (p. 11).

Ryle's suggestion is that it is only by concentrating on this kind of thinking that we can be led to imagine that thinking typically involves words with which one thinks.

Ryle challenges the intelligibility of the suggestion that we often think in words. He suggests that it may appear that we understand what it is to think in words

87

because we understand what it is for the Englishman to think in French, because we understand what it is to think about words, and because we understand what it is to record in words the stages of some calculation. But he points out that these cases are not sufficient to explain a sense of "think in" that makes intelligible what it is to think in words.

So we must examine this terminology in greater detail.

2. Mental states as tokens of sentences under analysis

What is a particular instance or a "token" of a sentence? Compare uttered and written tokens; tokens in different dialects, different handwriting, and different styles of type; and tokens uttered aloud and said to ourselves. What do all instances of a sentence have in common? At least two conditions seem necessary: (1) Any two tokens of the same sentence must have similar potential representational properties that, when placed in a context that reduces ambiguity and fixes reference, yield the actual representational properties. (2) Each token must be analyzable as an ordered sequence of the same words in the same order.

These conditions explain the difference between tokens of the same old sentences appearing in a new form (as the new written tokens compared with the older spoken tokens) and tokens of sentences in another language that translate sentences in the original language. In a language that can be both spoken and written, there is a corresponding written word for every possible spoken word. Every spoken sentence is a temporal sequence of spoken words; and the corresponding written sentence is a spatial sequence of corresponding written words in the same order, where corresponding written and spoken sentences have the same representational properties. This sort of general correspondence does not hold between distinct languages. We cannot, for example, correlate English and Russian words so that whenever a sequence of English words forms a sentence, the corresponding sequence of Russian words forms a sentence that translates the English sentence.

In chapter five I argued that an adequate account of mental states must treat them as having a kind of logical structure on which their representational characteristics depend, and I indicated that we might take mental states and thoughts to be tokens of sentences in a language of thought. My present claim is that the relation between some of these "sentences" and sentences in the language we speak is more like the relation between written and spoken English than like that between English and Russian. Of course, I do not suppose that the relevant thoughts and mental states are just strings of words. My claim is that they are tokens of sentences under analysis. In other words, I suggest that mental states can be taken to be structures of elements that are isomorphic to structures that are sentences under analysis, where the representational properties of the mental states correspond to those of the sentences under analysis.

The theory that mental states are sentences under analysis simplifies the theory of communication. To understand what is said is to perceive it as having an appropriate analysis. Given that perception of the sentence, communication is already successful; the speaker's thought was a token of the sentence under analysis, and the hearer's perception is another token of the same sentence under the same analysis. In the relevant sense, the speaker has communicated his thought to the hearer.

This theory also provides a simple account of ambiguity. Ambiguous sentences may be heard as having either of two (or more) different truth-conditional structures, like lines on paper that may be perceived as a staircase seen alternately from the back or front, like a group of dots that may be seen as two groups in one way or as two other groups in another way, or like the figure that can be seen either as a duck or as a rabbit. We may see or hear the sentence *they are visiting doctors* in two different ways, depending on whether we take *are visiting* together or *visiting doctors* together. We can hear the sentence as admitting either of two groups of paraphrases, either *they are doctors who are visiting* or *they are visiting some doctors*. Similarly, the different interpretations of *pleasing students can be boring* depends on how we conceive that sentence's grammatical structure, although this difference is not simply a matter of surface form. The difference is a matter of how we conceive the truth-conditional structural source of *pleasing students*, which may be heard as coming from *someone pleases students* or from *students please someone*.

It is true that the average person does not know any transformational grammar. But that does not mean that he fails to hear a sentence as having one or another of the indicated structures. A person can see lines on a page as forming one or another three-dimensional structure without knowing any geometry. In understanding what someone else says, we determine the content of his utterance taken literally. We assign a structure to the speaker's words in the sense that we hear his words as having a particular surface and underlying truth-conditional structure. That is not to say that we come (even unconsciously) to know that the sentence has that structure; and it is not to say that we have knowledge of the principles that relate phonetic representations to structural descriptions, for example. The situation is like other cases of perceiving something as something. We can perceive a series of lines as a particular three-dimensional structure without thinking that it has that structure, and without knowing rules that relate two-dimensional figures and three-dimensional structures.

When we see something as a three-dimensional structure, the structure need not be fully determinate. The exact relations among parts may be vague, and various details may not be specified at all. There are even two-dimensional figures that can be perceived as three-dimensional figures with a literally impossible structure. Similarly, perception of what is said is not always fully determinate. Certain aspects of structure may be left vague; and we can perceive double-talk as having an impossible structure. Thoughts and mental states can be like such perception of what has been said in being tokens of *partial* structures of sentences under analysis.

In learning a new language, we can usually understand what is said long before we can express ourselves in the language. This is true even in learning our first language. At first, the structures added to our system of mental representation are sufficiently incomplete so as not to include the full surface forms of sentences. That is why we are at first unable to think out loud in the language, even though we can perceive what someone says as having much of the structure it was intended to have.

3. Propositional attitudes versus sentential attitudes

I have argued that thoughts and mental states can be taken to be tokens of sentences under analysis, i.e., structures that involve surface forms of sentences coupled with their underlying truth-conditional structures. I have also argued that these structures may be indeterminate and may even be contradictory, as in the perception of double-talk. I have supposed that underlying truth-conditional structures are language-dependent in the sense that underlying predicates represent words in the language rather than universal concepts common to all language. I claim that the resulting theory helps to account for interaction between thought and language. In particular, it helps to explain how language makes thought possible, in that to acquire a language is to acquire a new system of representation to think in. It also simplifies the theory of normal linguistic communication in that to express thoughts in words is to think out loud. For the hearer to have the thought communicated, it is enough that he hear what is said as having the appropriate structure.

Philosophers have sometimes asked whether mental states should be construed as "sentential attitudes" or as "propositional attitudes." That is, they have asked whether being in a particular mental state (of belief, hope, fear, desire, etc.) should be identified with being in a relation of a certain sort to a sentence of a language or with being in a relation to a language-independent entity, a proposition, a meaning, or what is sometimes called a "semantic representation." It is not suggested that in any ordinary sense our attitudes are always attitudes toward sentences or propositions, as if whenever we were afraid we were afraid of a sentence or a proposition. The idea is rather that, e.g., fearing that Nixon will retire is to be analyzed as *fearing true* either the sentence *Nixon will retire* or the proposition that Nixon will retire. Believing, hoping, fearing, desiring, and so forth, are analyzed in terms of the relations believing-true, hoping-true, fearing-true, desiring-true, and so forth, where the issue is whether these relations relate a person either to a sentence or to a proposition.

I have suggested an intermediate position. According to me, certain mental states involve surface forms of sentences coupled with their language-dependent truth-conditional structures. These objects for neutral states are not just surface forms of sentences, nor are they propositions either, since unlike propositions they are specific to a language and even to particular sentences of the language, whereas propositions are not tied to any particular language.

Two sorts of objection might be raised against the view I am defending. One, discussed in chapter five, is that sentences are transformationally derived from language-independent underlying structures. I see no real arguments for this view. A second sort of objection is that our ordinary individuation of beliefs and other attitudes favors the theory of propositional attitudes over the sort of theory I am defending. This second objection is the more fundamental one; and it appears to lie behind the arguments of those who put forward the more syntactic objection. In the rest of this chapter I will try to say why I think that this objection is wrong.

4. Meanings

We ordinarily suppose that different sentences can express the same belief. We can account for some instances of our ordinary views about this by observing that different sentences have the same truth-conditional structure if they are what we might think of as transformational variants of each other. If *John hit Bob* and *Bob was hit by John* have the same underlying truth-conditional structure, these sentences can be taken to express what is the same thought except for its surface form. But what about *Bob is John's brother* and *Bob is John's male sibling*? Some philosophers and linguists have supposed that sentences like these can express the same thought or belief. To believe the one is to believe the other. How is that to be accounted for on my analysis? And what about the translation of one of these sentences into French? Cannot a Frenchman have the same belief I have when I believe that Bob is John's brother?

It is the beginning of a reply to observe that not all equivalent sentences can be transformationally derived from the same underlying structures. *John and Bob played golf* and *Bob and John played golf* are equivalent; but if they were to be derived from the same underlying structure, one or the other of *Bob* or *John* would have to come first; and either possibility is arbitrary. We might suggest that these elements are not ordered one before the other in underlying structure; but there are excellent reasons within the theory of grammar to suppose that elements of any structure to which transformational rules can apply are ordered with respect to each other.

So, we might say that *Bob is John's brother* and *Bob is John's male sibling* express equivalent thoughts or beliefs but not exactly the same thought or belief; and similarly with respect to their translations into French.

This, I repeat, is the beginning of a reply, but only the beginning, since the immediate rejoinder is that the relevant equivalences are linguistic, and not just empirical, so the theory of language must account for them. An account is available if we assume that sentences express linguistically independent meanings or propositions; but what sort of account is possible if that assumption is denied?

Indeed, this rejoinder can be put more generally. It will be said that there are facts about the use of language that can be explained in a natural way only if we suppose that all expressions have linguistically independent meanings that have certain interesting properties. For example, the meanings of parts of an expression may or may not fit together to yield a meaning of the larger expression. Thus, *quadruplicity drinks procrastination* is said to lack meaning because the meanings of its parts do not fit together; and *I threw a ball* is only two ways ambiguous even though both *threw* and *ball* are ambiguous because, on this theory, each meaning of *threw* fits together with only a single meaning of *ball*. This theory thus accounts for "semantic deviance" and "semantic disambiguation" by appeal to linguistically independent meanings. How else could we do so?

The same theory might also be supposed to account for the alleged distinction between truths that hold by virtue of meaning alone, the analytic truths, and those that depend also on facts about the world, the synthetic truths. (See chapter one, section 2.) The analytic truths include logical truths; truths that may not appear on the surface to be logical truths but that are seen to be logical truths when definitions of certain predicates are taken into account; and possibly also truths that follow logically from "meaning postulates," necessary principles that might be stated in an a priori theory of meaning and that are presupposed by any merely empirical theory.

This theory of meaning assumes that speakers of a language can in some sense introspect the meanings of sentences they use. According to the theory, that explains how they can semantically disambiguate sentences, tell that certain sentences are semantically deviant, and see that certain sentences are analytic truths. Furthermore, the theory implies that speakers use sentences to express thoughts that are in themselves linguistically neutral, so that the same thoughts might be expressed in different languages. There is on this view an important sense in which speakers of different languages think in a single language of thought. Some such theory lies behind the view of those linguists who assume that the theory of a language must associate sentences of the language with language independent "semantic representations."

5. *Dictionary definitions versus encyclopedia entries*

I claim that the theory of language-independent meanings or semantic representations is mistaken. It postulates a distinction that has no explanatory value. One way to put the point is to say that the theory assumes that an important distinction must be made between the entries in a person's internal dictionary and the entries in his internal encyclopedia; whereas I deny that there is any reason to believe that such a distinction can be made. A speaker's beliefs make up his encyclopedia. Some of these beliefs are more basic than others in that some are less easily given up or imagined false than others. But what is more or less basic is a matter of degree; it is a matter of what is more or less general and theoretical as well as a matter of what alternatives there might be to accepting one belief or another.

A speaker can determine that certain sentences are deviant, or weird. Can he distinguish semantic deviance from factual weirdness? Katz and Fodor suggest that the sentence, *this is silent paint*, is semantically deviant. But surely the weirdness of the sentence, if it is weird at all, comes from our general knowledge that paint does not make noise. If some paint gave off strange sounds and other paint did not, the sentence would no longer be weird. One might reply that this would lead to a change in the dictionary; but that just shows that no real distinction is to be made between dictionary and encyclopedia.

No purpose is served by thinking that certain principles available to a person are contained in his internal encyclopedia—and are therefore only synthetic—whereas other principles are part of his internal dictionary—and are therefore analytic. A man without an internal dictionary could include all the relevant principles in his internal encyclopedia. There would be no way to tell. He would just as firmly reject *quadruplicity drinks procrastination*, just as firmly deny *my brother is female*, and just as firmly assert *cats are animals*.

The same point holds for equivalence. Some underlying structures are equivalent to others by virtue of firmly held beliefs. These are not to be distinguished from underlying structures equivalent by virtue of a dictionary. There is no principled way to make out any such distinction. We can use an equivalence just as well whether it is to be found in one place or the other, the dictionary or the encyclopedia. In either case, it will have the same effect on behavior. The distinction between internal dictionaries and encyclopedias is a distinction that makes no difference.

The idea that there is an important epistemological distinction between dictionaries and encyclopedias does not survive a good look at a dictionary. Consider these examples from the *American Heritage Dictionary*: "cat: a carnivorous mammal, *Felis catus*, domesticated since early times as a catcher of rats and mice and as a pet, and existing in several distinctive breeds and varieties"; "elm: any of various deciduous trees of the genus *Ulmus*, characteristically having arching or curving branches and widely planted as shade trees." A picture of an elm tree and leaf is provided in the margin. The main difference between a dictionary and an encyclopedia is that dictionaries have more and shorter entries.

Philosophers have gone wrong by associating dictionary definitions with explicit definitions, which sometimes seem to *make* two expressions equivalent by virtue of meaning. For it seems that an explicitly defined equivalence cannot turn out to be false in the way that other equivalences can. If someone denies the equivalence, another retorts, "That's just the way I'm defining my terms." But that is because explicit definition is a kind of postulation. We postulate an equivalence. It is true that our postulates give meaning to our terms, because the meaning of those terms depends heavily on the beliefs we have or feign; and to postulate certain things is to believe them or feign a belief in them. Furthermore, immediately after postulates have been stated, it is inappropriate to challenge them. To state certain things as postulates is to say, "I shall assume these things." We then investigate the consequences of these assumptions. To challenge the assumptions is to do something else. Now, a definition can be one of the postulates (if we postulate an equivalence). If the definition is challenged, the response, "That's just the way I'm defining my terms" is a way of saying that we have postulated this equivalence. It is like saying, "This holds by hypothesis."

Later, after we have stopped just investigating the consequences of certain hypotheses, changes in theory may be called for. In that case we will just as readily change a postulate as anything else, even where we have postulated an equivalence in an explicit definition. This happens all the time in science, which is where explicit definition explicitly occurs. That something has been postulated to be true does not make it true. That something has been defined to be equivalent to something else does not make those things equivalent.

6. *Analyticity and witchcraft*

Defenders of linguistically independent meanings want to claim that there are certain intuitive distinctions that we are all able to make and that can be explained on their theory but not on a theory like the one I am proposing. Examples are the intuitive distinction between semantic deviance and factual weirdness, or the intuitive distinction between analytic and synthetic truths. In what follows, I shall concentrate on the analytic synthetic distinction; but it is easy to generalize what I say to cover semantic deviance versus factual weirdness.

Many people claim that, given a number of sentences, we can intuitively distinguish the analytic statements in them from the synthetic statements. Thus we will count as analytic statements statements like *my sister is a female, cats are animals,* and *a triangle has three angles* and will count as synthetic statements statements like *my sister is pretty, cats eat mice,* and *a triangle is not drawn on the blackboard.* To be sure, there may be borderline cases, like $5 + 7 = 12$ or *nothing that is red all over is also green all over at the same place at the same time.* But borderline cases do not undermine a distinction. Vague distinctions are still distinctions. There is a distinction between red and orange even though there is no sharp distinction between red and orange.

In fact it is doubtful that speakers of the language, *qua* speakers, make these distinctions. Training and indoctrination seem essential if we are to be able to make the distinction "correctly." Even then we may go wrong. Philosophers often disagree over cases.

Still, it will be said, speakers can be brought to make the distinction as soon as they learn what it is. After a few examples they are able to go on to give the right answers in a large number of other cases. We might even present a statistical analysis to show that after a small number of examples of analytic and synthetic sentences have been given, there is a highly significant agreement in the way further examples are classified.

This does show something, but only that speakers of a language can be taught philosophical theories. It shows that there is a distinction between what seems analytic and what seems synthetic to someone who accepts the analytic-synthetic distinction. However, we can distinguish between what seems analytic and what seems synthetic to those who accept this theory without supposing that any real distinction underlies the apparent one.

Once upon a time, women with supernatural powers, so-called witches, were distinguished from other women. We can admit that there is a distinction between women who seemed to be witches and women who did not seem to be witches to someone who believed in witches. But we should not go on to suppose that there really is a distinction between some women and others, some who have supernatural powers and others who do not. Nor do we have to believe that the women who would be called witches by believers in witchcraft all shared some common characteristic that other women lacked. For it may be and indeed is probably true that they would seem to have something in common only to someone who accepted the theory of witchcraft or to someone who attempted to look at them from the point of view of one who accepted the theory of witchcraft. For what they were thought to have in common was that they engaged in supernatural activities; various things could be taken to be evidence of that. E.g., perhaps one woman muttered in a strange way and then a cow died. Another seemed to prosper more than her neighbors. A third looked like some witches they burned at Easter. And so forth.

The analytic-synthetic distinction is like the witch-nonwitch distinction in that it presupposes a false view. Just as there are no real witches, there are no really analytic truths. Just as the women called witches turn out not to have anything in common, so too the so-called analytic truths have nothing in common that would distinguish them from other truths. Nothing, that is except their seeming to be analytic to someone who believes in the analytic-synthetic distinction.

Consider the variety of statements taken to be analytically true: statements concerning kinship relations like *a brother is a male sibling*; statements relating species and genus like *cats are animals*; statements connecting determinate and determinable like *red is a color*; statements of mathematics like $5 + 7 = 12$; statements of physical theory like $F = ma$; statements that certain relations are transitive or have converses like *if x is larger than y and y is larger than z, x is larger than z* and *if x is larger than y, y is smaller than x*; etc. What such truths have in common is that they have seemed analytic to someone who believed in analytic truth.

In order to get someone to distinguish analytic from synthetic truths, you must first convince him of a philosophical theory. The theory is that, although some statements are true by virtue of meaning and in addition by virtue of the way the world is, other statements are true by virtue of meaning alone. With statements of either sort, changing the meaning of their terms can make them false. But, if meaning is left fixed, changing the world might make statements of the first sort false but never statements of the second sort. Statements of the first sort owe their truth both to their meanings and to the world, whereas statements of the second sort owe their truth only to their meanings. They would be true no matter how the world were. Thus in some cases meaning is supposed to have a supernatural power to make statements true without any help at all from the world.

The evidence for this theory is that some people have great difficulty imagining certain things otherwise. Defenders of the analytic-synthetic distinction explain this difficulty by supposing that the things in question are true by virtue of meaning and so cannot be imagined false if meaning is kept constant. No matter what sort of world you imagine, it is claimed that an analytic statement will remain true in that world.

7. Against the supernatural

Now, to show that there is no distinction between witches and nonwitches, we must show that no women have supernatural powers. Similarly, to show that there is no real distinction between analytic and synthetic truths we need only to show that there are no meanings with supernatural powers.

In either area, two kinds of argument are possible. As for witches, we may argue that apparently clear cases of witches do not have the supernatural powers they are supposed to have, since if they are so powerful how are we able to keep them in the jail? If we come to doubt a sufficient number of particular cases, we will come to doubt whether there are any cases of witchcraft. A different sort of argument against witches comes from science. The notion of supernatural power does not fit in well with the rest of our conceptual scheme.

The same kinds of argument can be given about analyticity. Supposedly analytic truths can be seen to be false or at least imaginably false; and the notion of truth by virtue of meaning can be seen to be generally unscientific.

Analyticity is postulated to explain why we cannot imagine certain things not being true. A better postulate is that we are not good at imagining things. Kant thought that we could not imagine the falsity of Euclidean geometry. Einstein was able to do so. Kant's difficulty and Einstein's success are not to be explained by appeal to a difference in meaning. Nobody had worked out the details of a non-Euclidean geometry in Kant's time. No one saw how such a geometry could simplify our total theory until Einstein. Einstein was able to imagine things Kant could not.

What is interesting about the examples philosophers give of analytic truths is that so many of them are false. The explanation of why they cannot imagine their examples false is not, then, that the examples are analytically true. They cannot imagine their examples false because it does not occur to them to try.

A common example of a supposedly analytic statement is *bachelors are unmarried*. This shows how philosophy becomes tied to an outmoded morality. As nonphilosophers know, in this era of unstable marriages there are many bachelors who are still technically married. Another common example is *women are female*, although recently the Olympic Committee barred a woman from competition on the grounds that she had too many Y chromosomes to count as female.

It *is* true that cats are animals, another commonly cited analytic truth. But Putnam points out that inability to imagine this false is a matter of lack of imagination. Imagine the discovery that all of the furry things we've been calling cats are really made of plastic and are radio-controlled spy devices from Mars. What we have imagined is the discovery that cats are not animals. We can even imagine discovering that red is not a color but a smell, since we can imagine discovering that what we take to be the color red is perceived by smell rather than sight.

Of course, the failure of various examples does not by itself show that there is no analytic-synthetic distinction.

Being wrong about a few cases is no more disastrous for a defender of analyticity than for a defender of witch-craft. But, just as doubts about a large enough number of cases can lead to doubts about the witch-nonwitch distinction, doubts about a large enough number of supposedly analytic statements can lead to doubts about the distinction between analytic and synthetic statements. We become doubtful about supernatural powers.

Science presents a world view that allows no place for the supernatural. That undermines the witch-nonwitch distinction. Similarly, the distinction between analytic and synthetic truth is undermined by an account of the language-user that has no place for truth by virtue of meaning.

A language-user's beliefs instantiate sentences of his language under analysis. What his language is depends heavily on the sentences he believes; but there is no distinction between sentences under analysis that are accepted as true because of the meaning or semantic representation of the underlying structures and those that are accepted as true for some other reason. There are only sentences under analysis, more or less firmly accepted as true, more or less central to his conceptual scheme in the sense that it would be less or more easy to adapt to their loss.

There is no real distinction between change of language and change of view. In either case there is a change in the sentences under analysis we accept and/or a change in the connections between observation and these sentences. Some changes we may call changes in language, others changes in view. But there is no easy way to distinguish between these. Seeing why helps to eliminate the temptation to accept a distinction between analytic and synthetic truth.

There is an obvious connection here with translation. A change in the set of sentences under analysis that we accept counts as a change of view rather than a change in language to the extent that the best way to translate our earlier language into our later language is by mapping each sentence under analysis onto itself. If some other mapping yields a better translation, we speak of a change in language rather than a change in view.

8. Translation

This brings us to the central claim of those who postulate language-independent meanings or semantic representations, namely, that otherwise there is no account of translation. A given sentence under analysis in one language is supposed to translate a given sentence under analysis in another language if a meaning or semantic representation of the first is the same as one of the second. On this theory, there is a clear distinction between change in view and change in language. If we come to accept different sentences under analysis and the meanings or semantic representations associated with sentences do not change, that is change in view. If semantic representations change, that is change in language.

But in fact we can account for the possibility of translation without postulating linguistically neutral semantic representations. One general scheme of translation is better than another to the extent that it is simpler, preserves dispositions to accept sentences under analysis in response to observation, and preserves similarity in usage.[1] Each of these desiderata is a matter of degree, and they compete with each other. We could achieve perfect correspondence between another person's dispositions to accept sentences under analysis and our own if we were willing to give up on simplicity. And sometimes we do give up the simplest way to translate the sentences of a friend, i.e., the identity mapping, in order to preserve more of his dispositions to accept sentences under analysis or to gain more similarity in actual usage. The fit is never perfect; but let us assume that there is sometimes a unique best fit: a best general scheme of translation.

The fit is only a matter of degree, so the translation relation need not be transitive. If x is the translation of y and y is the translation of z, x may not be the translation of z. There may be three languages L, M, and N, such that the best scheme of translation from L to N is not equivalent to what we get by first translating by the best scheme from L to M and then by the best scheme from M to N. This tells against the suggestion that translation should pair sentences under analysis that have the same semantic representations, since if x and y have the same semantic representation and y and z have the same semantic representation, x and z must have the same semantic representation.

Proponents of the analytic-synthetic distinction claim that we cannot give up basic analytic principles without changing the meaning of our words. This presupposes

[1] Where similarity in usage must be understood to cover "genetic factors." (See chapter four, n. 2.)

a real distinction between changing our view and only appearing to change it by changing the meaning of words used to state it. But that distinction is only a matter of degree. Any change of belief can be considered a change in meaning in the sense that it makes the identity-mapping somewhat less good a scheme of translation. A sufficient number of small changes done in a systematic way can add up to a large enough change so that the simplicity of the identity-mapping is outweighed by the preservation of dispositions to accept sentences and of actual usage that would be gained by switching to an alternative scheme. No one change by itself brings about a change in meaning; but together they all do. We cannot suppose that the resulting overt change in meaning is the result of our having given up some analytically true belief, for then we could find the point at which the change in meaning occurred.

Two people can be said to mean exactly the same thing by their words if the identity-translation works perfectly to preserve dispositions to accept sentences under analysis and actual usage. To the extent that the identity-translation does not work perfectly, people do not mean *exactly* the same thing by their words; but if the identity-translation is better than alternatives we will say that they mean the same thing by their words. Here we mean by *the same, roughly the same* rather than *exactly the same*, as when we say that two red books are the same color although it is clear that they are not exactly the same in color. The only sort of sameness of meaning we know is similarity in meaning, not exact sameness of meaning. This is where the defender of the

109

analytic-synthetic distinction has gone wrong; he confuses a similarity relationship with an equivalence relationship.

9. Conclusion

This does not absolutely refute the analytic-synthetic distinction any more than science absolutely refutes someone who believes in witches. But it shows that there is a plausible view of language which has no place for truth by virtue of meaning and thus no place for linguistically neutral semantic representations. It is open to a defender of analyticity to reply, e.g., that the canons of good translation are not necessary and sufficient conditions of good translation but are instead principles of evidence. Then the puzzle about transitivity I have offered becomes a version of the lottery paradox discussed in chapter seven, section 2. There can be good evidence that x is the translation of y and also good evidence that y is the translation of z and also good evidence that x is not the translation of z. The truth of the matter, it could be said, depends on what is meant by x, y, and z. Some people still believe in witches.

Meaning is not a matter of language-independent meanings. It is a matter of the functional role in the language of thought of sentences of our outer language under analysis. An important aspect of that role, noted in chapter four, section 4, is role with respect to evidence and inference. Evidential and inferential role depends, of course, on a background of firmly accepted beliefs and goals. Meaning is therefore partly a matter of what is firmly accepted; but there is no real distinction between meaning postulates and others or between change in view and in meaning.

To complete this picture of the mental life, we must return to our study of reasoning, for reasoning is a process that produces changes in our beliefs and goals, thereby determining the functional role of sentences in the language of thought. Therefore, in the remaining chapters of this book we take up again the idea that we can use intuitions about when people know things in order to learn about inference and reasoning.

Chapter 7

Knowledge and Probability

1. Knowledge, belief, truth, and justification

Recall that one response to skepticism assumes the validity of certain principles of justification and then tries to use those principles to refute the skeptic by arguing that we are justified in believing many of the things we ordinarily suppose we know. The major problem with any such response is that it merely transfers the skeptical challenge to the assumed principles of justification (chapter one, sections 1-3). A better idea does not attempt to "answer" skepticism at all. Instead the idea is to turn skepticism on its head and use intuitive judgments about when people know things to discover when reasoning occurs and what its principles are (chapter one, sections 4-5). Making use of the latter strategy, I have argued that reasons which give a person knowledge derive from reasoning that occurs as a largely unconscious nondeterministic mental process (chapter two, 1-3; chapter three, 6-7). For several chapters I have been elaborating an account of mental states and processes that allows for this sort of reasoning and explains the failure of the analytic-synthetic distinction. I now want to return to my original strategy in order to bring out important aspects of principles of reasoning.

Care must be taken in appealing to what is ordinarily *said* as evidence concerning ordinary judgments about knowledge. For example, an American citizen may have said (in 1971), "I don't *believe* that Nixon is president, I *know* that Nixon is president." That this could be said might be offered as evidence that knowledge does not always imply belief. This would be a mistake, since the same speaker might have said, "Nixon isn't *an* elected official, he's the *president*," without meaning to deny that the presidency is an elective office. We account for both remarks by supposing that intonation and emphasis here indicate a suppressed, "merely": "I don't merely *believe* that Nixon is president, I *know* that Nixon is president," "Nixon isn't merely *an* elected official, he's the *president*."

Another example that might be taken to show that knowledge does not always imply belief occurs in the remark, "I know that Nixon is president, but I don't believe it." This remark involves a special use of the word "believe," since in one sense the speaker does believe that Nixon is president and in another sense he does not. To believe something in the second sense is to be able to bear the thought of it. Knowledge implies belief but not always in the sense that one can bear the thought of what it is one believes.

Here is a harder example to evaluate (from Radford). Mabel asks George when the Declaration of Independence was signed. George is unsure and "guesses" 1776 (the right answer), although he has no confidence in his answer. Let us suppose that he once learned the answer and in some sense retained it in memory, which is why

113

his "guess" is correct. It might be argued that it would be appropriate to describe George as knowing but not believing that the Declaration of Independence was signed in 1776. But is this so? It seems clear that in such a case George does not believe that his answer is correct; but on the other hand it also seems clear that he does not know that his answer is correct. Perhaps he knows that the Declaration of Independence was signed in 1776; but, then, doesn't he believe that that is when the Declaration of Independence was signed? He can believe it without realizing that he does. So this fails to be a clear case in which there is knowledge without belief. Perhaps it is clear that George does know that the Declaration of Independence was signed in 1776 and does not believe that his answer is correct. But that is not to know something that he does not believe. For we can reasonably suggest both that he believes that the Declaration of Independence was signed in 1776 and that he does not know that his answer is correct. Where he knows, he believes; where he does not believe, he does not know.

Or consider the claim that knowledge implies truth. It is no objection that people sometimes say that they know things that turn out not to be so. The Romans thought that they knew that the earth is flat. That does not mean the Roman conception of knowledge permitted knowledge of something that wasn't so. The Romans believed that it was true that the earth is flat. Had they come to believe that it was false, they would have ceased believing that they knew or had ever known that the earth is flat. We can confirm that knowledge implies truth by examining ordinary usage without having to assume that every remark or belief concerning knowledge is correct.

It is sometimes objected that if knowledge implied truth, knowledge would be unattainable. But that assumes that truth is unattainable, which is a misconception about truth. All that is needed for the truth of the belief that the earth is round is that the earth should be round. If John believes that the earth is round and George believes that the earth is not round, then it follows logically that either John or George has attained truth. For one or the other has a true belief; and that is what is meant when it is said that knowledge implies truth: what is believed must be true. To say that we can know the earth is round only if it is true that the earth is round is only to say that we can know this only if the earth is round. That knowledge implies truth is not by itself an argument for skepticism.

Another claim often made about the ordinary concept of knowledge is that we can know something only if we are justified in believing it. A problem with such a claim is that it is unclear when we are justified in believing something. We can know something without being able to produce a justification in the form of an argument for it. For sometimes knowledge is not based on any reasons at all, as when one knows that one has a headache; and even when knowledge is based on reasons, one may not be able to produce those reasons in any detail (chapter two, section 2). Furthermore, the reasons that give one knowledge need not be reasons for which one believes as one does (chapter two, 3; chapter ten, 5).

The problem is compounded when we consider knowledge acquired some time ago. I know that Colum-

bus discovered America in 1492 but it is not obvious
that there are any reasons for which I now believe this,
although there once were. I continue to believe that Co-
lumbus discovered America in 1492, having forgotten
how I ever learned it. It is clear that I *have* some reason
to think my belief is true, namely, the fact that I believe
it. For if I believe it, I must have learned it; and why
would anyone have taught it to me unless it were true?
But I can have reasons for believing something that are
not the reasons for which I believe it (chapter two, section 1). It is not obvious that the reasoning just cited
would specify reasons for which I believe that Colum-
bus discovered America in 1492, since the reasoning
presupposes that very belief. For the same reason it is
obscure how such reasoning could be said to support
my belief, for that is like saying that the belief supports
itself. On the other hand, perhaps, I am justified in continuing to believe something like this in the absence of
reasons against it.

I shall postpone further discussion of this problem to
the final chapter, which discusses memory and knowledge. Until then I will concentrate on cases of coming
to know something; in dealing with those cases I will
apply the strategy of using intuitive judgments about
when people know things in order to discover principles
of reasoning that justify belief.

Here is one example of the use of that strategy. Unger
suggests that a man might come to know something he
sees in a crystal ball, if the ball works, even though it is
irrational for him to believe what he sees. But why
should we assume that it is irrational for him to believe
the ball? I deny that there is any way to discover such

116

irrationality except by way of intuitive judgments about when people come to know things. So, if we are inclined to say a man could come to know something he sees in the crystal ball, it follows that he could be justified in believing what he sees.

What could his justification be? To answer that is to anticipate later discussion, but we can say this. He is justified in believing that there is some connection between the events represented in the ball and their representation in the ball. The connection might be that the events are responsible for the representation (as would be true if the ball is part of a closed-circuit television system) or that the representation is responsible for the occurrence of the events (as would be true if the owner of the ball sets out to make true whatever his clients see in the ball). A man might be justified in believing what he sees in the ball even though he does not know what the connection is and even if in some sense he thinks that belief in the ball is irrational. The test is whether in some such circumstance we would be willing to say that he knows. Similarly, a man who does not understand the mechanism of vision and who has been "convinced" of philosophical skepticism concerning the senses is nevertheless justified in believing what he sees, since it is appropriate to say of him that he comes to know things through vision despite his philosophical view.

Again, this is to anticipate later discussion. The subject is justification and principles of inference, and I want to begin at a simpler level. It is often suggested that justification has something to do with probability, so I will now pause to explore that suggestion.

117

2. *The lottery paradox*

Some philosophers argue that we never simply believe anything that we do not take to be certain. Instead we believe it to a greater or lesser degree; we assign it a higher or lower "subjective probability." If knowledge implies belief, on this view we never know anything that isn't absolutely certain. That conflicts with ordinary views about knowledge, since our degree of belief in some things we think we know is greater than our degree of belief in other things we think we know.

We might count as believed anything whose "subjective probability" exceeds .99. But that would also conflict with ordinary views. We do not suppose that a man inconsistently believes of every participant in a fair lottery that the participant will lose, even though we suppose that the man assigns a subjective probability greater than .99 to each person's losing. If ordinary views are to be preserved, belief must be distinguished from high degree of belief.

A rule of inductive inference is sometimes called a "rule of acceptance," since it tells us what we can accept (i.e., believe), given other beliefs, degrees of belief, etc. A purely probabilistic rule of acceptance says that we may accept something if and only if its probability is greater than .99. Kyburg points out that such a rule leads to a "lottery paradox" since it authorizes the acceptance of an inconsistent set of beliefs, each saying of a particular participant in a lottery that he will lose.

It is true that no contradiction arises if conclusions are added to the evidence on whose basis probabilities are calculated. Concluding that a particular person will lose changes the evidential probability that the next person will lose. When there are only 100 people left, we cannot infer the next person will lose, since the evidential probability of this no longer exceeds .99. But this does not eliminate paradox. The paradox is not just that use of a purely probabilistic rule leads to inconsistent beliefs. It is not obviously irrational to have inconsistent beliefs even when we know that they are inconsistent. It has occasionally been suggested[1] that a rational man believes that he has at least some (other) false beliefs. If so, it follows logically that at least one thing he believes *is* false (if nothing else, then his belief that he has other false beliefs); a rational man will know that. So a rational man knows that at least one thing he believes is false. Nevertheless it *is* paradoxical to suppose that we could rationally believe of every participant in a lottery that he will lose; and it is just as paradoxical to suppose that we could rationally believe this of all but 100 participants in a large lottery.

The lottery paradox can be avoided if a purely probabilistic rule of acceptance is taken to be relevant not to the acceptance of various individual hypotheses but rather to the set of what we accept. The idea is that the probability of the whole set must exceed .99. We are free to choose among various hypotheses saying that one or another participant in a lottery loses as long as the probability of the conjunction of all hypotheses accepted remains above .99. (The idea requires a distinction between what is simply accepted and what is accepted as evidence. If we could add new conclusions to the evidence, the lottery paradox would be generated

---

[1] E.g., by Robert Nozick.

as indicated in the previous paragraph.) However, although this version of a purely probabilistic rule does not yield the lottery paradox, it does not fit in with ordinary views, as I shall now argue.

3. Gettier examples and probabilistic rules of acceptance

In any Gettier example we are presented with similar cases in which someone infers h from things he knows, h is true, and he is equally justified in making the inference in either case. In the one case he comes to know that h and in the other case he does not. I have observed that a natural explanation of many Gettier examples is that the relevant inference involves not only the final conclusion h but also at least one intermediate conclusion true in the one case but not in the other. And I have suggested that any account of inductive inference should show why such intermediate conclusions are essentially involved in the relevant inferences. Gettier cases are thus to be explained by appeal to the principle

P Reasoning that essentially involves false conclusions, intermediate or final, cannot give one knowledge (chapter three, section 6).

It is easy to see that purely probabilistic rules of acceptance do not permit an explanation of Gettier examples by means of principle P. Reasoning in accordance with a purely probabilistic rule involves essentially only its final conclusion. Since that conclusion is highly probable, it can be inferred without reference to any other conclusions; in particular, there will be no intermediate conclusion essential to the inference that is true in one case and false in the other.

For example, Mary's friend Mr. Nogot convinces her that he has a Ford. He tells her that he owns a Ford, he shows her his ownership certificate, and he reminds her that she saw him drive up in a Ford. On the basis of this and similar evidence, Mary concludes that Mr. Nogot owns a Ford. From that she infers that one of her friends owns a Ford. In a normal case, Mary might in this way come to know that one of her friends owns a Ford. However, as it turns out in this case, Mary is wrong about Nogot. His car has just been repossessed and towed away. It is no longer his. On the other hand, Mary's friend Mr. Havit does own a Ford, so she is right in thinking that one of her friends owns a Ford. However, she does not realize that Havit owns a Ford. Indeed, she hasn't been given the slightest reason to think that he owns a Ford. It is false that Mr. Nogot owns a Ford, but it is true that one of Mary's friends owns a Ford. Mary has a justified true belief that one of her friends owns a Ford but she does not know that one of her friends owns a Ford. She does not know this because principle P has been violated. Mary's reasoning essentially involves the false conclusion that Mr. Nogot owns a Ford.[2]

But, if there were probabilistic rules of acceptance, there would be no way to exhibit the relevance of Mary's intermediate conclusion. For Mary could then have inferred her final conclusion (that one of her friends owns a Ford) directly from her original evi-

[2] Lehrer (1965).

dence, all of which is true. Mr. Nogot *is* her friend, he *did* say he owns a Ford, he *did* show Mary an ownership certificate, she *did* see him drive up in a Ford, etc. If a purely probabilistic rule would permit Mary to infer from that evidence that her friend Nogot owns a Ford, it would also permit her to infer directly that one of her friends owns a Ford, since the latter conclusion is at least as probable on the evidence as the former. Given a purely probabilistic rule of acceptance, Mary need not first infer an intermediate conclusion and then deduce her final conclusion, since by means of such a rule she could directly infer her final conclusion. The intermediate conclusion would not be essential to her inference, and her failure to know that one of her friends owns a Ford could not be explained by appeal to principle *P*.

A defender of purely probabilistic rules might reply that what has gone wrong in this case is not that Mary *must* infer her conclusion from something false but rather that, from the evidence that supports her conclusion, she *could* also infer something false, namely that Mr. Nogot owns a Ford. In terms of principle *P*, this would be to count as essential to Mary's inference any conclusion the probabilistic rule would authorize from her starting point. But given any evidence, some false conclusion will be highly probable on that evidence. This follows, e.g., from the existence of lotteries. For example, let *s* be a conclusion saying under what conditions the New Jersey State Lottery was most recently held. Let *q* say what ticket won the grand prize. Then consider the conclusion, *not both s and q*. Call that conclusion *r*. The conclusion *r* is highly probable, given evidence having nothing to do with the outcome of the recent lottery, but *r* is false. If such highly probable false conclusions were always considered essential to an inference, Mary could never come to know anything.

The problem is that purely probabilistic considerations do not suffice to account for the peculiar relevance of Mary's conclusion about Nogot. Various principles might be suggested; but none of them work. For example, we might suspect that the trouble with *r* is that it has nothing to do with whether any of Mary's friends owns a Ford. Even if Mary were to assume that *r* is false, her original conclusion would continue to be highly probable on her evidence. So we might suggest that an inferable conclusion *t* is essential to an inference only if the assumption that *t* was false would block the inference. That would distinguish Mary's relevant intermediate conclusion, that Nogot owns a Ford, from the irrelevant conclusion *r*, since if Mary assumed that Nogot does not own a Ford she could not conclude that one of her friends owns a Ford.

But again, if there is a purely probabilistic rule of acceptance, there will always be an inferable false *t* such that the assumption that it is false would block even inferences that give us knowledge. For let *h* be the conclusion of any inference not concerned with the New Jersey Lottery and let *r* be as above. Then we can let *t* be the conjunction *h&r*. This *t* is highly probable on the same evidence *e* on which *h* is highly probable; *t* is false; and *h* is not highly probable relative to the evidence *e&(not t)*. Any inference would be undermined by such a *t*, given a purely probabilistic rule of acceptance along with the suggested criterion of essential conclusions.

The trouble is that purely probabilistic rules are incompatible with the natural account of Gettier examples by means of principle *P*. The solution is not to attempt to modify *P* but rather to modify our account of inference.

4. Summary

My strategy is to appeal to ordinary judgments about knowledge in order to discover what the principles of inference are. Appeal to ordinary judgments requires a certain amount of care; we cannot simply read off answers to philosophical questions from what people say. But it does seem possible to appeal to such judgments in order to confirm that knowledge implies true belief and, at least in a restricted range of cases, involves being justified in believing as we do.

In this chapter I have been particularly concerned with probability, in particular with whether justification can be accounted for in purely probabilistic terms. I have suggested a negative answer. First, there is the lottery paradox. A purely probabilistic rule of acceptance would permit us to infer of every or almost every participant in a lottery that he will lose, and that seems paradoxical. Second, there are the Gettier examples. One can have justified true belief and fail to know, if a conclusion essential to one's inference is false; but there seems to be no plausible way to explain what it is for a conclusion to be essential to one's inference if there is a purely probabilistic rule of acceptance.

In what follows I will therefore approach the subject in a different way. I will propose a different and more plausible account of inference that avoids the lottery paradox and is compatible with the natural explanation of the Gettier examples by means of principle *P*.

Chapter **8**

Knowledge and Explanation

1. A causal theory

Goldman suggests that we know only if there is the proper sort of causal connection between our belief and what we know. For example, we perceive that there has been an automobile accident only if the accident is relevantly causally responsible, by way of our sense organs, for our belief that there has been an accident. Similarly, we remember doing something only if having done it is relevantly causally responsible for our current memory of having done it. Although in some cases the fact that we know thus simply begins a causal chain that leads to our belief, in other cases the causal connection is more complicated. If Mary learns that Mr. Havit owns a Ford, Havit's past ownership is causally responsible for the evidence she has and also responsible (at least in part) for Havit's present ownership. Here the relevant causal connection consists in there being a common cause of the belief and of the state of affairs believed in.

Mary fails to know in the original Nogot-Havit case because the causal connection is lacking. Nogot's past ownership is responsible for her evidence but is not responsible for the fact that one of her friends owns a Ford. Havit's past ownership at least partly accounts for why one of her friends now owns a Ford, but it is not responsible for her evidence. Similarly, the man who is told something true by a speaker who does not believe what he says fails to know because the truth of what is said is not causally responsible for the fact that it is said.

General knowledge does not fit into this simple framework. That all emeralds are green neither causes nor is caused by the existence of the particular green emeralds examined when we come to know that all emeralds are green. Goldman handles such examples by counting logical connections among the causal connections. The belief that all emeralds are green is, in an extended sense, relevantly causally connected to the fact that all emeralds are green, since the evidence causes the belief and is logically entailed by what is believed.

It is obvious that not every causal connection, especially in this extended sense, is relevant to knowledge. Any two states of affairs are logically connected simply because both are entailed by their conjunction. If every such connection were relevant, the analysis Goldman suggests would have us identify knowledge with true belief, since there would always be a relevant "causal connection" between any state of true belief and the state of affairs believed in. Goldman avoids this reduction of his analysis to justified true belief by saying that when knowledge is based on inference relevant causal connections must be "reconstructed" in the inference. Mary knows that one of her friends owns a Ford only if her inference reconstructs the relevant causal connection between evidence and conclusion.

But what does it mean to say that her inference must

127

"reconstruct" the relevant causal connection? Presumably it means that she must infer or be able to infer something about the causal connection between her conclusion and the evidence for it. And this suggests that Mary must make at least two inferences. First she must infer her original conclusion and second she must infer something about the causal connection between the conclusion and her evidence. Her second conclusion is her "reconstruction" of the causal connection. But how detailed must her reconstruction be? If she must reconstruct every detail of the causal connection between evidence and conclusion, she will never gain knowledge by way of inference. If she need only reconstruct some "causal connection," she will always know, since she will always be able to infer that evidence and conclusion are both entailed by their conjunction.

I suggest that it is a mistake to approach the problem as a problem about what else Mary needs to infer before she has knowledge of her original conclusion. Goldman's remark about reconstructing the causal connection makes more sense as a remark about the kind of inference Mary needs to reach her original conclusion in the first place. It has something to do with principle P and the natural account of the Gettier examples.

Nogot presents Mary with evidence that he owns a Ford. She infers that one of her friends owns a Ford. She is justified in reaching that conclusion and it is true. However, since it is true, not because Nogot owns a Ford, but because Havit does, Mary fails to come to know that one of her friends owns a Ford. The natural explanation is that she must infer that Nogot owns a

Ford and does not know her final conclusion unless her intermediate conclusion is true. According to this natural explanation, Mary's inference essentially involves the conclusion that Nogot owns a Ford. According to Goldman, her inference essentially involves a conclusion concerning a causal connection. In order to put these ideas together, we must turn Goldman's theory of knowledge into a theory of inference.

As a first approximation, let us take his remarks about causal connections literally, forgetting for the moment that they include logical connections. Then let us transmute his causal theory of knowing into the theory that inductive conclusions always take the form X *causes* Y, where further conclusions are reached by additional steps of inductive or deductive reasoning. In particular, we may deduce either X or Y from X *causes* Y.

This causal theory of inferring provides the following account of why knowledge requires that we be right about an appropriate causal connection. A person knows by inference only if all conclusions essential to that inference are true. That is, his inference must satisfy principle P. Since he can legitimately infer his conclusion only if he can first infer certain causal statements, he can know only if he is right about the causal connection expressed by those statements. First, Mary infers that her evidence is a causal result of Nogot's past ownership of the Ford. From that she deduces that Nogot has owned a Ford. Then she infers that his past ownership has been causally responsible for present ownership; and she deduces that Nogot owns a Ford. Finally, she deduces that one of her friends owns a

129

Ford. She fails to know because she is wrong when she infers that Nogot's past ownership is responsible for Nogot's present ownership.

2. Inference to the best explanatory statement

A better account of inference emerges if we replace "cause" with "because." On the revised account, we infer not just statements of the form X *causes* Y but, more generally, statements of the form Y *because* X or X *explains* Y. Inductive inference is conceived as inference to the best of competing explanatory statements. Inference to a causal explanation is a special case.

The revised account squares better with ordinary usage. Nogot's past ownership helps to explain Mary's evidence, but it would sound odd to say that it caused that evidence. Similarly, the detective infers that activities of the butler explain these footprints; does he infer that those activities caused the footprints? A scientist explains the properties of water by means of a hypothesis about unobservable particles that make up the water, but it does not seem right to say that facts about those particles cause the properties of water. An observer infers that certain mental states best explain someone's behavior; but such explanation by reasons might not be causal explanation (chapter three, section 7).

Furthermore, the switch from "cause" to "because" avoids Goldman's *ad hoc* treatment of knowledge of generalizations. Although there is no causal relation between a generalization and those observed instances which provide us with evidence for the generalization, there is an obvious explanatory relationship. That all emeralds are green does not cause a particular emerald to be green; but it can explain why that emerald is green. And, other things being equal, we can infer a generalization only if it provides the most plausible way to explain our evidence.

We often infer generalizations that explain but do not logically entail their instances, since they are of the form, *In circumstances C, X's tend to be Y's.* Such generalizations may be inferred if they provide a sufficiently plausible account of observed instances all things considered. For example, from the fact that doctors have generally been right in the past when they have said that someone is going to get measles, I infer that doctors can normally tell from certain symptoms that someone is going to get measles. More precisely, I infer that doctors have generally been right in the past because they can normally tell from certain symptoms that someone is going to get measles. This is a very weak explanation, but it is a genuine one. Compare it with the pseudo-explanation, "Doctors are generally right when they say someone has measles because they can normally tell from certain symptoms that someone is going to get measles."

Similarly, I infer that a substance is soluble in water from the fact that it dissolved when I stirred it into some water. That is a real explanation, to be distinguished from the pseudo-explanation, "That substance dissolves in water because it is soluble in water." Here too a generalization explains an instance without entailing that instance, since water-soluble substances do not always dissolve in water.

131

Although we cannot simply deduce instances from this sort of generalization, we can often infer that the generalization will explain some new instance. The inference is warranted if the explanatory claim *that X's tend to be Y's will explain why the next X will be Y* is sufficiently more plausible than competitors such as *interfering factor Q will prevent the next X from being a Y*. For example, the doctor says that you will get measles. Because doctors are normally right about that sort of thing, I infer that you will. More precisely, I infer that doctors' normally being able to tell when someone will get measles will explain the doctor's being right in this case. The competing explanatory statements here are not other explanations of the doctor's being right but rather explanations of his being wrong—e.g., because he has misperceived the symptoms, or because you have faked the symptoms of measles, or because these symptoms are the result of some other disease, etc. Similarly, I infer that this sugar will dissolve in my tea. That is, I infer that the solubility of sugar in tea will explain this sugar's dissolving in the present case. Competing explanations would explain the sugar's not dissolving—e.g., because there is already a saturated sugar solution there, because the tea is ice-cold, etc.

3. Further examples[1]

I infer that when I scratch this match it will light. My evidence is that this is a Sure-Fire brand match, and in the past Sure-Fire matches have always lit when scratched. However, unbeknownst to me, this particular

[1] Skyrms.

match is defective. It will not light unless its surface temperature can be raised to six hundred degrees, which is more than can be attained by scratching. Fortunately, as I scratch the match, a burst of Q-radiation (from the sun) strikes the tip, raising surface temperature to six hundred degrees and igniting the match. Did I know that the match would light? Presumably I did not know. I had justified true belief, but not knowledge. On the present account, the explanation of my failure to know is this: I infer that the match will light in the next instance because Sure-Fire matches generally light when scratched. I am wrong about that; that is not why the match will light this time. Therefore, I do not know that it will light.

It is important that our justification can appeal to a simple generalization even when we have false views about the explanation of that generalization. Consider the man who thinks that barometers fall before a rainstorm because of an increase in the force of gravity. He thinks the gravity pulls the mercury down the tube and then, when the force is great enough, pulls rain out of the sky. Although he is wrong about this explanation, the man in question can come to know that it is going to rain when he sees the barometer falling in a particular case. That a man's belief is based on an inference that cannot give him knowledge (because it infers a false explanation) does not mean that it is not also based on an inference that does give him knowledge (because it infers a true explanation). The man in question has knowledge because he infers not only the stronger explanation involving gravity but also the weaker explanation. He infers that the explanation of the past correlation between falling barometer and rain is that the falling barometer is normally associated with rain. Then he infers that this weak generalization will be what will explain the correlation between the falling barometer and rain in the next instance.

Notice that if the man is wrong about that last point, because the barometer is broken and is leaking mercury, so that it is just a coincidence that rain is correlated with the falling barometer in the next instance, he does not come to know that it is going to rain.

Another example is the mad-fiend case. Omar falls down drunk in the street. An hour later he suffers a fatal heart attack not connected with his recent drinking. After another hour a mad fiend comes down the street, spies Omar lying in the gutter, cuts off his head, and runs away. Some time later still, you walk down the street, see Omar lying there, and observe that his head has been cut off. You infer that Omar is dead; and in this way you come to know that he is dead. Now there is no causal connection between Omar's being dead and his head's having been cut off. The fact that Omar is dead is not causally responsible for his head's having been cut off, since if he had not suffered that fatal heart attack he still would have been lying there drunk when the mad fiend came along. And having his head cut off did not cause Omar's death, since he was already dead. Nor is there a straightforward logical connection between Omar's being dead and his having his head cut off. (Given the right sorts of tubes, one might survive decapitation.) So it is doubtful that Goldman's causal theory of knowing can account for your knowledge that Omar is dead.

If inductive inference is inference to the best explanatory statement, your inference might be parsed as follows: "Normally, if someone's head is cut off, that person is dead. This generalization accounts for the fact that Omar's having his head cut off is correlated here with Omar's being dead." Relevant competing explanatory statements in this case would not be competing explanations of Omar's being dead. Instead they would seek to explain Omar's not being dead despite his head's having been cut off. One possibility would be that doctors have carefully connected head and body with special tubes so that blood and air get from body to head and back again. You rule out that hypothesis on grounds of explanatory complications: too many questions left unanswered (why can't you see the tubes? why wasn't it done in the hospital? etc.). If you cannot rule such possibilities out, then you cannot come to know that Omar is dead. And if you do rule them out but they turn out to be true, again you do not come to know. For example, if it is all an elaborate psychological philosophical experiment, which however fails, then you do not come to know that Omar is dead even though he is dead.

4. Statistical inference

Statistical inference, and knowledge obtained from it, is also better explicated by way of the notion of statistical explanation than by way of the notion of cause or logical entailment. A person may infer that a particular coin is biased because that provides the best statistical explanation of the observed fraction of heads. His conclusion explains his evidence but neither causes nor entails it.

The relevant kind of statistical explanation does not always make what it explains very probable. For example, suppose that I want to know whether I have the fair coin or the weighted coin. It is equally likely that I have either; the probability of getting heads on a toss of the fair coin is 1/2; and the probability of getting heads on a toss of the weighted coin is 6/10. I toss the coin 10,000 times. It comes up heads 4,983 times and tails 5,017. I correctly conclude that the coin is the fair one. You would ordinarily think that I could in this way come to know that I have the fair coin. On the theory of inference we have adopted, I infer the best explanation of the observed distribution of heads and tails. But the explanation, that these were randon tosses of a fair coin, does not make it probable that the coin comes up heads exactly 4,983 times and tails exactly 5,017 times in 10,000 tosses. The probability of this happening with a fair coin is very small. If we want to accept the idea that inference is inference to the best explanatory statement, we must agree that statistical explanation can cite an explanation that makes what it explains less probable than it makes its denial. In the present case, I do not explain why 4,983 heads have come up rather than some other number of heads. Instead I explain how it happened that 4,983 heads came up, what led to this happening. I do not explain why this happened rather than something else, since the same thing could easily have led to something else.

To return to an earlier example (chapter three, section 7), you walk into a casino and see the roulette wheel stop at red fifty times in a row. The explanation may be that the wheel is fixed. It may also be that the wheel is fair and this is one of those times when fifty reds come up on a fair wheel. Given a fair wheel we may expect that to happen sometimes (but not very often). But if the explanation is that the wheel is fair and that this is just one of those times, it says what the sequence of reds is the result of, the "outcome" of. It does not say why fifty reds in a row occurred this time rather than some other time, nor why that particular series occurred rather than any of the $2^{50}-1$ other possible series.

This kind of statistical explanation explains something as the outcome of a chance set-up. The statistical probability of getting the explained outcome is irrelevant to whether or not we explain that outcome, since this kind of explanation is essentially pure nondeterministic explanation. All that is relevant is that the outcome to be explained is one possible outcome given that chance set-up. That is not to say that the statistical probability of an outcome is irrelevant to the explanation of that outcome. It is relevant in this sense: the greater the statistical probability an observed outcome has in a particular chance set-up, the better that set-up explains that outcome.

The point is less a point about statistical explanation than a point about statistical inference. I wish to infer the best of competing statistical explanations of the observed distribution of heads. This observed outcome has different statistical probabilities in the two hypothetical chance set-ups, fair coin or weighted coin. The higher this statistical probability, the better, from the point of view of inference (other things being equal). The statistical probability of an outcome in a particular hypothetical chance set-up is relevant to how good an explanation that chance set-up provides. Here a better explanation is one that is more likely to be inferable. For example, I infer that I have the fair coin. The statistical probability of 4,983 heads on 10,000 tosses of a fair coin is much greater than the statistical probability of that number of heads on 10,000 tosses of the weighted coin. From the point of view of statistical probability, the hypothesis that the coin is fair offers a better explanation of the observed distribution than the hypothesis that the coin is biased. So statistical probability is relevant to statistical explanation. Not that there is no explanation unless statistical probability is greater than $1/2$. Rather that statistical probability provides a measure of the inferability of a statistical explanation.

According to probability theory, if initially the coin is just as likely to be the fair one or the weighted one and the statistical probability of the observed outcome is much greater for the fair coin than for the weighted coin, the probability that the coin is fair, given the observed evidence, will be very high. We might conclude that the statistical probability of the observed outcome given the fair or weighted coin is only indirectly relevant to my inference, relevant only because of the theoretical connections between those statistical probabilities and the evidential probabilities of the two hypotheses about the coin, given the observed evidence. But that would be to get things exactly backward. No doubt there is a connection between high evidential probability and inference; but, as we have seen, it is not because there is a purely probabilistic rule of acceptance (chapter seven, section 3). High probability by itself does not warrant inference. Only explanatory considerations can do that; and the probability relevant to explanation is statistical probability, the probability that is involved in statistical explanation. It is the statistical probabilities of the observed outcome, given the fair and weighted coins, that is directly relevant to inference. The evidential probabilities of the two hypotheses are only indirectly relevant in that they in some sense reflect the inferability of the hypotheses, where that is determined directly by considerations of statistical probability.

Suppose that at first you do not know which of the two coins I have selected. I toss it 10,000 times, getting 4,983 heads and 5,017 tails. You infer that I have the fair coin, and you are right. But the reason for the 4,983 heads is that I am very good at tossing coins to come up whichever way I desire and I deliberately tossed the coin so as to get roughly half heads and half tails. So, even though you have justified true belief, you do not know that I have the fair coin.

If statistical inference were merely a matter of inferring something that has a high probability on the evidence, there would be no way to account for this sort of Gettier example. And if we are to appeal to principle P, it must be a conclusion essential to your inference that the observed outcome is the result of a chance set-up involving the fair coin in such a way that the probability of heads is $1/2$. Given a purely probabilistic rule, that conclusion could not be essential, for reasons similar to those that have already been discussed concerning the Nogot-Havit case (chapter seven, section 3). On the other hand, if statistical inference is inference to the best explanation and there is such a thing as statistical explanation even where the statistical probability of what is explained is quite low, then your conclusion about the reason for my getting 4,983 heads is seen to be essential to your inference. Since your explanation of the observed outcome is false, principle P accounts for the fact that you do not come to know that the coin is the fair coin even though you have justified true belief.

5. Conclusion

We are led to construe induction as inference to the best explanation, or more precisely as inference to the best of competing explanatory statements. The conclusion of any single step of such inference is always of the form Y *because* X (or X *explains* Y), from which we may deduce either X or Y. Inductive reasoning is seen to consist in a sequence of such explanatory conclusions.

We have been led to this conception of induction in an attempt to account for Gettier examples that show something wrong with the idea that knowledge is justified true belief. We have tried to find principles of inference which, together with principle P, would explain Gettier's deviant cases. Purely probabilistic rules were easily seen to be inadequate. Goldman's causal theory of knowing, which promised answers to some of Gettier's questions, suggested a causal theory of induction: inductive inference as inference to the best of competing causal statements. Our present version is simply a modification of that, with *explanatory* replacing *causal*. Its strength lies in the fact that it accounts for a variety of inferences, including inferences that involve weak generalizations or statistical hypotheses, in a way that explains Gettier examples by means of principle P.

Chapter 9

Evidence One Does Not
Possess

1. Three examples

Example (1). While I am watching him, Tom takes a library book from the shelf and conceals it beneath his coat. Since I am the library detective, I follow him as he walks brazenly past the guard at the front door. Outside I see him take out the book and smile. As I approach he notices me and suddenly runs away. But I am sure that it was Tom, for I know him well. I saw Tom steal a book from the library and that is the testimony I give before the University Judicial Council. After testifying, I leave the hearing room and return to my post in the library. Later that day, Tom's mother testifies that Tom has an identical twin, Buck. Tom, she says, was thousands of miles away at the time of the theft. She hopes that Buck did not do it; but she admits that he has a bad character.

Do I know that Tom stole the book? Let us suppose that I am right. It was Tom that took the book. His mother was lying when she said that Tom was thousands of miles away. I do not know that she was lying, of course, since I do not know anything about her, even that she exists. Nor does anyone at the hearing know that she is lying, although some may suspect that she is. In these circumstances I do not know that Tom stole the book. My knowledge is undermined by evidence I do not possess.[1]

EXAMPLE (2). Donald has gone off to Italy. He told you ahead of time that he was going; and you saw him off at the airport. He said he was to stay for the entire summer. That was in June. It is now July. Then you might know that he is in Italy. It is the sort of thing one often claims to know. However, for reasons of his own Donald wants you to believe that he is not in Italy but in California. He writes several letters saying that he has gone to San Francisco and has decided to stay there for the summer. He wants you to think that these letters were written by him in San Francisco, so he sends them to someone he knows there and has that person mail them to you with a San Francisco postmark, one at a time. You have been out of town for a couple of days and have not read any of the letters. You are now standing before the pile of mail that arrived while you were away. Two of the phony letters are in the pile. You are about to open your mail. I ask you, "Do you know where Donald is?" "Yes," you reply, "I know that he is in Italy." You are right about where Donald is and it would seem that your justification for believing that Donald is in Italy makes no reference to letters from San Francisco. But you do not know that Donald is in Italy. Your knowledge is undermined by evidence you do not as yet possess.

EXAMPLE (3). A political leader is assassinated. His associates, fearing a coup, decide to pretend that

---

[1] Lehrer and Paxson.

the bullet hit someone else. On nationwide television they announce that an assassination attempt has failed to kill the leader but has killed a secret service man by mistake. However, before the announcement is made, an enterprising reporter on the scene telephones the real story to his newspaper, which has included the story in its final edition. Jill buys a copy of that paper and reads the story of the assassination. What she reads is true and so are her assumptions about how the story came to be in the paper. The reporter, whose by-line appears, saw the assassination and dictated his report, which is now printed just as he dictated it. Jill has justified true belief and, it would seem, all her intermediate conclusions are true. But she does not know that the political leader has been assassinated. For everyone else has heard about the televised announcement. They may also have seen the story in the paper and, perhaps, do not know what to believe; and it is highly implausible that Jill should know simply because she lacks evidence everyone else has. Jill does not know. Her knowledge is undermined by evidence she does not possess.

These examples pose a problem for my strategy. They are Gettier examples and my strategy is to make assumptions about inference that will account for Gettier examples by means of principle P. But these particular examples appear to bring in considerations that have nothing to do with conclusions essential to the inference on which belief is based.

Some readers may have trouble evaluating these examples. Like other Gettier examples, these require attention to subtle facts about ordinary usage; it is easy to miss subtle differences if, as in the present instance, it is very difficult to formulate a theory that would account for these differences. We must compare what it would be natural to say about these cases if there were no additional evidence one does not possess (no testimony from Tom's mother, no letters from San Francisco, and no televised announcement) with what it would be natural to say about the cases in which there is the additional evidence one does not possess. We must take care not to adopt a very skeptical attitude nor become too lenient about what is to count as knowledge. If we become skeptically inclined, we will deny there is knowledge in either case. If we become too lenient, we will allow that there is knowledge in both cases. It is tempting to go in one or the other of these directions, toward skepticism or leniency, because it proves so difficult to see what general principles are involved that would mark the difference. But at least some difference between the cases is revealed by the fact that we are *more inclined* to say that there is knowledge in the examples where there is no undermining evidence a person does not possess than in the examples where there is such evidence. The problem, then, is to account for this difference in our inclination to ascribe knowledge to someone.

2. *Evidence against what one knows*

If I had known about Tom's mother's testimony, I would not have been justified in thinking that it was Tom I saw steal the book. Once you read the letters from Donald in which he says he is in San Francisco, you are no longer justified in thinking that he is in Italy. If Jill knew about the television announcement, she would not be justified in believing that the political leader has been assassinated. This suggests that we can account for the preceding examples by means of the following principle.

One knows only if there is no evidence such that if one knew about the evidence one would not be justified in believing one's conclusion.

However, by modifying the three examples it can be shown that this principle is too strong.

Suppose that Tom's mother was known to the Judicial Council as a pathological liar. Everyone at the hearing realizes that Buck, Tom's supposed twin, is a figment of her imagination. When she testifies no one believes her. Back at my post in the library, I still know nothing of Tom's mother or her testimony. In such a case, my knowledge would not be undermined by her testimony; but if I were told only that she had just testified that Tom has a twin brother and was himself thousands of miles away from the scene of the crime at the time the book was stolen, I would no longer be justified in believing as I now do that Tom stole the book. Here I know even though there is evidence which, if I knew about it, would cause me not to be justified in believing my conclusion.

Suppose that Donald had changed his mind and never mailed the letters to San Francisco. Then those letters no longer undermine your knowledge. But it is very difficult to see what principle accounts for this fact. How can letters in the pile on the table in front of you undermine your knowledge while the same letters in a pile in front of Donald do not? If you knew that Donald had written letters to you saying that he was in San Francisco, you would not be justified in believing that he was still in Italy. But that fact by itself does not undermine your present knowledge that he is in Italy.

Suppose that as the political leader's associates are about to make their announcement, a saboteur cuts the wire leading to the television transmitter. The announcement is therefore heard only by those in the studio, all of whom are parties to the deception. Jill reads the real story in the newspaper as before. Now, she does come to know that the political leader has been assassinated. But if she had known that it had been announced that he was not assassinated, she would not have been justified in believing that he has, simply on the basis of the newspaper story. Here, a cut wire makes the difference between evidence that undermines knowledge and evidence that does not undermine knowledge.

We can know that h even though there is evidence e that we do not know about such that, if we did know about e, we would not be justified in believing h. If we know that h, it does not follow that we know that there is not any evidence like e. This can seem paradoxical, for it can seem obvious that, if we know that h, we know that any evidence against h can only be misleading. So, later if we get that evidence we ought to be able to know enough to disregard it.

147

A more explicit version of this interesting paradox goes like this.[2] "If I know that h is true, I know that any evidence against h is evidence against something that is true; so I know that such evidence is misleading. But I should disregard evidence that I know is misleading. So, once I know that h is true, I am in a position to disregard any future evidence that seems to tell against h." This is paradoxical, because I am never in a position simply to disregard any future evidence even though I do know a great many different things.

A skeptic might appeal to this paradox in order to argue that, since we are never in a position to disregard any further evidence, we never know anything. Some philosophers would turn the argument around to say that, since we often know things, we are often in a position to disregard further evidence. But both of these responses go wrong in accepting the paradoxical argument in the first place.

I can know that Tom stole a book from the library without being able automatically to disregard evidence to the contrary. You can know that Donald is in Italy without having the right to ignore whatever further evidence may turn up. Jill may know that the political leader has been assassinated even though she would cease to know this if told that there was an announcement that only a secret service agent had been shot.

The argument for paradox overlooks the way actually having evidence can make a difference. Since I now know that Tom stole the book, I now know that any evi-

---

[2] Here and in what follows I am indebted to Saul Kripke, who is, however, not responsible for any faults in my presentation.

dence that appears to indicate something else is misleading. That does not warrant me in simply disregarding any further evidence, since getting that further evidence can change what I know. In particular, after I get such further evidence I may no longer know that it is misleading. For having the new evidence can make it true that I no longer know that Tom stole the book; if I no longer know that, I no longer know that the new evidence is misleading.

Therefore, we cannot account for the problems posed by evidence one does not possess by appeal to the principle, which I now repeat:

One knows only if there is no evidence such that if one knew about the evidence one would not be justified in believing one's conclusion.

For one can know even though such evidence exists.

3. A result concerning inference

When does evidence one doesn't have keep one from having knowledge? I have described three cases, each in two versions, in which there is misleading evidence one does not possess. In the first version of each case the misleading evidence undermines someone's knowledge. In the second version it does not. What makes the difference?

My strategy is to account for Gettier examples by means of principle P. This strategy has led us to conceive of induction as inference to the best explanation. But that conception of inference does not by itself seem able to explain these examples. So I want to use the examples in order to learn something more about inference, in particular about what other conclusions are essential to the inference that Tom stole the book, that Donald is in Italy, or that the political leader has been assassinated.

It is not plausible that the relevant inferences should contain essential intermediate conclusions that refer explicitly to Tom's mother, to letters from San Francisco, or to special television programs. For it is very likely that there is an infinite number of ways a particular inference might be undermined by misleading evidence one does not possess. If there must be a separate essential conclusion ruling out each of these ways, inferences would have to be infinitely inclusive—and that is implausible.

Therefore it would seem that the relevant inferences must rule out undermining evidence one does not possess by means of a single conclusion, essential to the inference, that characterizes all such evidence. But how might this be done? It is not at all clear what distinguishes evidence that undermines knowledge from evidence that does not. How is my inference to involve an essential conclusion that rules out Tom's mother's testifying a certain way before a believing audience but does not rule out (simply) her testifying in that way? Or that rules out the existence of letters of a particular sort in the mail on your table but not simply the existence of those letters? Or that rules out a widely heard announcement of a certain sort without simply ruling out the announcement?

Since I am unable to formulate criteria that would distinguish among these cases, I will simply *label* cases of the first kind "undermining evidence one does not possess." Then we can say this: one knows only if there is no undermining evidence one does not possess. If there is such evidence, one does not know. However, these remarks are completely trivial.

It is somewhat less trivial to use the same label to formulate a principle concerned with inference.

Q One may infer a conclusion only if one also infers that there is no undermining evidence one does not possess.

There is of course an obscurity in principle *Q*; but the principle is not as trivial as the remarks of the last paragraph, since the label "undermining evidence one does not possess" has been explained in terms of knowledge, whereas this is a principle concerning inference.

If we can explain "undermining" without appeal to knowledge, given *Q*, we can use principle *P* to account for the differences between the two versions of each of the three examples described above. In each case an inference involves essentially the claim that there is no undermining evidence one does not possess. Since this claim is false in the first version of each case and true in the second, principle *P* implies that there can be knowledge only in the second version of each case.

So there is, according to my strategy, some reason to think that there is a principle concerning inference like principle *Q*. That raises the question of whether there is any independent reason to accept such a principle; and reflection on good scientific practice suggests a positive answer. It is a commonplace that a scientist should base his conclusions on all the evidence. Furthermore, he should not rest content with the evidence he happens to have but should try to make sure he is not overlooking any relevant evidence. A good scientist will not accept a conclusion unless he has some reason to think that there is no as yet undiscovered evidence which would undermine his conclusion. Otherwise he would not be warranted in making his inference. So good scientific practice reflects the acceptance of something like principle Q, which is the independent confirmation we wanted for the existence of this principle.

Notice that the scientist must accept something like principle Q, with its reference to "undermining evidence one does not possess." For example, he cannot accept the following principle,

> One may infer a conclusion only if one also infers that there is no evidence at all such that if he knew that evidence he could not accept his conclusion.

There will always be a true proposition such that if he learned that the proposition was true (and learned nothing else) he would not be warranted in accepting his conclusion. If h is his conclusion, and if k is a true proposition saying what ticket will win the grand prize in the next New Jersey State Lottery, then *either k or not h* is such a proposition. If he were to learn that it is true that *either k or not h* (and learned nothing else), *not h* would become probable since (given what he knows) k is antecedently very improbable. So he could no longer reasonably infer that h is true.

152

There must be a certain kind of evidence such that the scientist infers there is no as yet undiscovered evidence of that kind against *h*. Principle *Q* says that the relevant kind is what I have been labelling "undermining evidence one does not possess." Principle *Q* is confirmed by the fact that good scientific practice involves some such principle and by the fact that principle *Q* together with principle *P* accounts for the three Gettier examples I have been discussing.

If this account in terms of principles *P* and *Q* is accepted, inductive conclusions must involve some self-reference. Otherwise there would be a regress. Before we could infer that *h*, we would have to infer that there is no undermining evidence to *h*. That prior inference could not be deductive, so it would have to be inference to the best explanatory statement. For example, we might infer that the fact that there is no sign of undermining evidence we do not possess is explained by there not being any such evidence. But, then, before we could accept that conclusion we would first have to infer that there is no undermining evidence to *it* which one does not possess. And, since that inference would have to be inference to the best explanation, it would require a previous inference that there is no undermining evidence for its conclusion; and so on *ad infinitum*.

Clearly, we do not *first* have to infer that there is no undermining evidence to *h* and only then infer *h*. For that would automatically yield the regress. Instead, we must at the same time infer both *h* and that there is no undermining evidence. Furthermore, we infer that there is not only no undermining evidence to *h* but also no undermining evidence to the whole conclusion. In other words, all legitimate inductive conclusions take the form of a self-referential conjunction whose first conjunct is h and whose second conjunct (usually left implicit) is the claim that there is no undermining evidence to the whole conjunction.

Chapter **10**

Conclusions as Total Views

1. Problems

In chapter eight we saw that we could use principle *P* to account for many Gettier examples if we were willing to suppose that induction always has an explanatory statement as its conclusion. On that supposition reasoning would have to take the form of a series of inductive and deductive steps to appropriate intermediate conclusions that therefore become essential to our inference. However, certain difficulties indicate that this conception of inference is seriously oversimplified and that our account of Gettier examples must be modified.

Chapter nine has already mentioned a minor complication. There is a self-referential aspect to inductive conclusions. Instead of saying that such conclusions are of the form *Y because X* we must say that they are of the form *Y because X and there is no undermining evidence to this whole conclusion.*

Another difficulty, mentioned in chapter seven, section 2, the "lottery paradox," poses a more serious problem. Recall that this paradox arises given a purely probabilistic rule of acceptance, since such a rule would have us infer concerning any ticket in the next New Jersey lottery that the ticket will not win the grand prize.

We might suggest that the paradox cannot arise if induction is inference to the best explanatory statement, since the hypothesis that a particular ticket fails to win the grand prize in the next New Jersey lottery does nothing to explain anything about our current evidence. However, there are two things wrong with such a suggestion. First, the paradox will arise in any situation in which, for some large number N, there are N different explanations of different aspects of the evidence, each inferable when considered apart from the other explanations, if we also know that only $N - 1$ of these explanations are correct. So, the paradox can arise even when we attempt to infer explanations of various aspects of one's evidence.

Furthermore, inference to the best explanatory statement need not infer explanations of the evidence. It can infer that something we already accept will explain something else. That is how I am able to infer that the sugar will dissolve when stirred into my tea or that a friend who intends to meet me on a corner in an hour will in fact be there (chapter eight, section 2). Moreover, we can sometimes infer explanatory statements involving statistical explanations; and, if a particular ticket does fail to win the grand prize, we can explain its not winning by describing this as a highly probable outcome in the given chance set-up (chapter eight, section 4). So, if induction is inference to the best explanatory statement, we should be able to infer of any ticket in a fair lottery that the conditions of the lottery will explain that ticket's failing to win the grand prize; the lottery paradox therefore arises in its original form. But before attempting to modify the present conception of inference in order to escape the lottery paradox, let us consider a different sort of problem involving that conception.

Our present conception of reasoning takes it to consist in a series of inductive and deductive steps. We have therefore supposed that there are (at least) two kinds of inference, inductive inference and deductive inference; and we have also supposed that reasoning typically combines inferences of both sorts. But there is something fishy about this. Deduction does not seem to be a kind of inference in the same sense in which induction is. Induction is a matter of inductive acceptance (chapter seven, section 2). On our current conception of inference, we may infer or accept an explanatory statement if it is sufficiently more plausible than competing statements, given our antecedent beliefs. On the other hand, deduction does not seem in the same way to be a matter of "deductive acceptance." So called deductive rules of inference are not plausibly construed as rules of deductive acceptance that tell us what conclusions we may accept, given that we already have certain antecedent beliefs. For example, although the deductive rule of *modus ponens* is sometimes stated like this, "From *P* and *If P, then Q,* infer *Q*," there is no plausible rule of acceptance saying that if we believe both *P* and *If P, then Q,* we may always infer or accept *Q*. Perhaps we should stop believing *P* or *If P, then Q* rather than believe *Q*.

A contradiction logically implies everything; anything follows (deductively) from a set of logically inconsistent beliefs. Although this point is sometimes expressed by saying that from a contradiction we may deductively infer anything, that is a peculiar use of "infer." Logic does not tell us that if we discover that our beliefs are inconsistent we may go on to infer or accept anything and everything we may happen to think of. Given the discovery of such inconsistency in our antecedent beliefs, inference should lead not to the acceptance of something more but to the rejection of something previously accepted.

This indicates that something is wrong in a very basic way with our current conception of inference. We have been supposing that inference is simply a way to acquire new beliefs on the basis of our old beliefs. What is needed is a modification of that conception to allow for the fact that inference can lead as easily to rejection of old beliefs as to the acceptance of new beliefs. Furthermore, we want to avoid the supposition that deduction is a kind of inference in the same sense in which induction is inference, and we want to avoid the lottery paradox.

2. Inference to the best total explanatory account

Influenced by a misleading conception of deductive inference, we have implicitly supposed that inductive inference is a matter of going from a few premises we already accept to a conclusion one comes to accept, of the form X *because* Y *(and there is no undermining evidence to this conclusion)*. But this conception of premises and conclusion in inductive inference is mistaken. The conception of the conclusion of induction is wrong since such inference can lead not only to the acceptance of new beliefs but also the rejection of old beliefs. Furthermore, the suggestion that only a few premises are relevant is wrong, since inductive inference must be assessed with respect to everything one believes.

A more accurate conception of inductive inference takes it to be a way of modifying what we believe by addition and subtraction of beliefs. Our "premises" are all our antecedent beliefs; our "conclusion" is our total resulting view. Our conclusion is not a simple explanatory statement but a more or less complete explanatory account. Induction is an attempt to increase the explanatory coherence of our view, making it more complete, less ad hoc, more plausible. At the same time we are conservative. We seek to minimize change. We attempt to make the least change in our antecedent view that will maximize explanatory coherence.

The conception of induction as inference to the best total explanatory account retains those aspects of our previous conception that permitted an account of Gettier examples, although that account must be modified to some extent (as noted in section 5). On the other hand, the new conception does not suppose that there is deductive inference in anything like the sense in which there is inductive inference, since deductive inference is not a process of changing beliefs. Furthermore, the new conception accounts for the fact that inference can lead us to reject something previously accepted, since such rejection can be part of the least change that maximizes coherence.

Finally, the new conception avoids the lottery paradox. Inference is no longer conceived of as a series of steps which together might add up to something implausible as a whole. Instead, inference is taken to be a

159

single step to one total conclusion. If there can be only one conclusion, there is no way to build up a lottery paradox.

Consider the case in which there are N explanations of various aspects of the evidence, each very plausible considered by itself, where however it is known that only $N - 1$ are correct. Competing possible conclusions must specify for each explanation whether or not that explanation is accepted. A particular explanation will be accepted not simply because of its plausibility when considered by itself but only if it is included in an inferable total explanatory account. We will not be able to infer that all N explanations are correct since, I am assuming, that would greatly decrease coherence.

Similarly, we will be able to infer that a particular ticket will fail to win the grand prize in the next New Jersey lottery only if there is a total resulting view containing this result that is to be preferred to alternative total views on grounds of maximizing coherence and minimizing change. The claim that a particular ticket fails to win will be part of an inferable total view only if that claim adds sufficiently more coherence than do claims that other tickets fail to win. Otherwise that total view will not be any better than a different total view that does not contain the claim that the first ticket fails to win.

This is a rather complicated matter and depends not only on the probabilities involved but also on how we conceive the situation and, in particular, on what claims we are interested in.[1] We can see this by considering the conditions under which we can make inferences that give us knowledge. For example, if we are simply inter-

[1] Levi.

ested in the question of whether a particular ticket will win or fail to win, we cannot include in our total view the conclusion that the ticket will fail to win, since it would not be correct to say that in such a case we know the ticket will lose. On the other hand, if we are primarily interested in a quite different question whose answer depends in part on an answer to the question of whether this ticket fails to win, we may be able to include the conclusion that it does fail in our total view, since we can often come to have relevant knowledge in such cases. Thus, we might infer and come to know that the butler is the murderer because that hypothesis is part of the most plausible total account, even though the account includes the claim that the butler did not win the lottery (for if he had won he would have lacked a motive). Or we might infer and come to know that we will be seeing Jones for lunch tomorrow even though our total view includes the claim that Jones does not win the lottery (e.g., because if he won he would have to be in Trenton tomorrow to receive his prize and would not be able to meet us for lunch).

However I am unable to be very precise about how our interests and conception of the situation affect coherence or indeed about any of the factors that are relevant to coherence.

3. Deduction and explanation

Deductive logic is a theory of logical implication (chapter five, section 2). It is concerned with "arguments" and "proofs," but in technical senses of these words. An argument in this sense consists of a set of "premises" and a "conclusion." The argument is "valid" if the premises logically imply the conclusion. A proof in the technical sense consists of a number of steps of argument whose conclusions are logically implied by "axioms," which are specified in advance, together with any previous conclusions, each step being in accordance with a set of rules of logical implication, also specified in advance.

Arguments in this sense must be distinguished from inferences or instances of reasoning. Although rules of logical implication are sometimes called "rules of inference," that is a misnomer. Deductive arguments and proofs are not inferences in the way that inductive inferences are. Nor are inductive inferences arguments that fail to provide the sort of absolute proof that deductive arguments provide. There are neither inductive arguments nor deductive inferences. There are only deductive arguments and inductive inferences.

It is true that reasons can often be stated in the form of a deductive argument. But that does not mean that inference or reasoning is an argument. It means that deductive arguments have something to do with explanatory coherence. An argument is not an inference, but it may be part of a conclusion. When, as we say, someone reasons *P, Q, R; so S*, it is not just that he believes *P, Q,* and *R,* and comes as a result to believe *S*. He comes to believe *S, because P, Q, and R.*

Any valid deductive argument explains its conclusion in the sense that it states a reason why that conclusion is true. Of course, it will not state the only reason and we are often much more interested in the reason given by some other explanation. For example, we often wish to know not just a reason why it is true that something

162

happened but a reason why it happened, an explanation of what caused, produced, or led up to its happening. To say, "Jack is the murderer, because the murderer is the man with size 13 feet and Jack has size 13 feet," may be to give a reason why it is true that Jack is a murderer without giving a reason why Jack is a murderer. To give the latter sort of reason is to say something about what led to Jack's being a murderer; and his having size 13 feet may have nothing to do with that.

Some deductive arguments may seem to be too trivial to be explanations. Consider "Jack killed George, because Jack killed George and Jack killed Harry," or even "Jack killed George, because Jack killed George." These do not seem to explain anything. But they are not much in the way of arguments either; and, just as it simplifies the theory of deductive arguments to count them as trivial arguments, it also simplifies the theory of explanation to count them as trivial explanations.

(It is unlikely that we could characterize the notion of a trivial or question-begging argument in a purely formal way, within the theory of deductive logic. The triviality or question-begging character of an argument has to do with its not yielding sufficient explanatory coherence to make its conclusion acceptable. That is a matter of standards of inference rather than rules of logic.)

4. Logic and inference

The idea that deductive argument is inference can have disastrous philosophical consequences. For instance, it can lend support to certain skeptical arguments and then to implausible philosophical theories put forward to combat those skeptical arguments. If we suppose that beliefs are to be justified by deducing them from more basic beliefs, we will suppose that there are beliefs so basic that they cannot be justified at all. To avoid the conclusion that these must just be taken on faith, we may suggest that they can be seen to be true by direct and immediate intuition, perhaps by virtue of our knowledge of the language (chapter one, section 3; chapter six, 6-7).

In ethics this line of thought leads to relativism and "noncognitivism." Noncognitivism is the idea that we can never know any moral truths, because there is no way to derive our basic moral principles from anything else, because there is no such thing as direct awareness of basic moral truths, and because it is a fallacy (the "naturalistic fallacy") to suppose that knowledge of meaning can tell us anything interesting about morality. Relativism is the view that everyone has his own ultimate principles, which differ from person to person in such a way that no one can show his principles to be more justified than anyone else's.

These skeptical views are undermined (or at least take different forms) once it is seen that the relevant kind of justification is not a matter of derivation from basic principles but is rather a matter of showing that a view fits in well with other things we believe. This kind of justification works as well for general principles as for specific points.

The mistaken idea that deductive logic is the logic of deductive inference can also lead to the conclusion that there is a subject of inductive logic, the logic of inductive inference. Then, seeing that deduction has to do with deductive relations like logical implication, we may go on to suppose that induction must have something to do with inductive relations, which we may identify with probabilistic relations. Therefore we may conclude that inductive logic has something to do with the theory of probability.

For example, it is a truism that inductive conclusions must be assessed with respect to our total evidence. If we believe in inductive logic, we may think this truism is to be explicated in terms of the notion of conditional probability, where the conditional probability of a hypothesis h, given evidence e, is defined to be the prior probability of the conjunction $h\&e$ divided by the prior probability of the evidence e. Thus we will suppose that inductive conclusions should have a high probability conditional on the total evidence, as just defined.

An obvious difficulty with this supposition is that, no matter how evidence is interpreted, induction sometimes tells us to reject some of the evidence. That is, to reject something that has probability 1 on the total evidence and to accept something that has probability 0, where 1 is the highest possible probability and 0 is the lowest possible probability. For in such a case we reject an h that is logically implied by e and accept *not h*. The prior probability of $h\&e$ will be the same as that of e, since logical equivalents have the same probability and in such a case e is logically equivalent to $h\&e$. The prior probability of *(not h)*$\&e$ will be 0, since it is logically false and logical falsehoods have a probability of 0. The conditional probability of h given e is the prior probability of *h&e* divided by that of *e*, so it is 1. The conditional probability of *not h* given *e* is the prior probability of *(not h)&e* divided by that of *e*, so it is 0. Yet one rejects *h* and accepts *not h*.

Some philosophers seek to evade this argument by distinguishing beliefs accepted as evidence from other beliefs accepted but not as evidence.[2] They say that conditional probability on the total evidence in the technical sense is relevant only in deciding questions of simple acceptance or rejection. In deciding whether to change what we accept as evidence, they say that we must appeal to (unspecified) considerations that are different from those relevant to simple acceptance or rejection. In particular, these other considerations would not appeal to conditional probability on the total evidence.

But that is a mere evasion, an ad hoc attempt to rescue an assumption based on a mistaken analogy between induction and deduction. The principles used in accepting or rejecting beliefs as evidence are not to be distinguished from those used in accepting or rejecting any other beliefs. We always make the least change that maximizes explanatory coherence. There is no distinction between what we accept as evidence and whatever else we accept.

The total-evidence requirement does not say that inductive conclusions are to be evaluated in the light of their conditional probability, given something labeled "total evidence." It says rather that induction is inference to the best total explanatory account. The whole view is relevant, not because all of it is accepted as un-

[2] E.g., Levi.

challengeable evidence (since any part of the view might be rejected) but because all the view must be taken into account.

The probabilistic interpretation of the principle of total evidence is only one example of the many ways we can be misled by the idea that there is a logic of inductive inference. Another example is the suggestion, discussed above (in chapter seven, sections 2-3), that there is a purely probabilistic rule of acceptance. The suggestion is apparently based on the thought that, just as the deductive relation of logical implication warrants acceptance of the conclusion of a deductive inference, a sufficiently strong inductive relation of probabilistic implication can warrant acceptance of the conclusion of an inductive inference.

It is true that, just as deductive arguments involving a relation of logical implication can be relevant to the coherence of a view (section 3), probabilities can also be relevant to coherence. For example, the statistical probabilities the observed evidence has on various hypotheses can be relevant to the inferability of those hypotheses (chapter eight, section 4). But this provides no reason to think of probability theory as an inductive logic.

The deductive relation of logical implication is a matter of truth and of logical form (chapter five, section 2). Probabilistic relations are not just a matter of truth and form, so there is no reason to take them to be logical relations even if we say that the logic is inductive rather than deductive. The logic of probability theory is not inductive logic; it is the same old deductive logic that applies everywhere else. In stating the theory of proba-

167

bility we state some axioms which logically imply the theorems we want in the same old sense of "logically imply." Deductive logic is the only logic there is.

Let me add here that considerations similar to those that lead to talk of inductive logic can also lead to talk of a logic of practical reasoning. Thus we will notice that there is such a thing as practical reasoning which is not reducible to what we think of as deductive reasoning. So we will conclude that what is needed is a practical or imperative logic over and above deductive logic.

This is not the place for a full-scale account of practical reasoning; but it should be clear that the account will have nothing to do with a new kind of *logic*. In practical reasoning we begin with a set of beliefs and goals and end with a new set, where we try to maximize coherence and minimize change. In this case coherence is not just a matter of explanatory coherence in our beliefs but also involves coherence in our plans. I am not sure how to be more specific than this, to say something that preserves the relevant distinction between predicting and deciding. However that is to be done, it will not involve any sort of practical logic.

5. Inference and knowledge

Having seen that induction is inference to the best total explanatory account, we must now modify our account of knowledge and of the Gettier examples.

One problem is that we want to be able to ascribe several inferences to a person at a particular time so as to be able to say that one of the inferences yields knowledge even though another does not. Suppose that Mary has evidence both that her friend Mr. Nogot owns a Ford and that her friend Mr. Havit owns a Ford. She concludes that both own Fords and therefore that at least one of her friends owns a Ford. Nogot does not own a Ford; but Havit does. We want to be able to say that Mary can know in this case that at least one of her friends owns a Ford, because one inference on which her belief is based satisfies principle P even if another inference she makes does not. But, if inference is a matter of modifying one's total view, how can we ascribe more than a single inference to Mary?[3]

Principle P seems to be in trouble in any event. It tells us that one gets knowledge from an inference only if all conclusions essential to that inference are true. Since one's conclusion is one's total resulting view, principle P would seem to imply that one gains no knowledge from inference unless the whole of one's resulting view is true. But that is absurd. A person comes to know things through inference even though some of what he believes is false.

A similar point holds of premises. It is plausible to suppose that one comes to know by inference only if one already knows one's premises to be true. However, one's total view is relevant to inference even though it always contains things one does not know to be true.

The key to the solution of these problems is to take an inference to be a change that can be described simply by mentioning what beliefs are given up and what new beliefs are added (in addition to the belief that there is no undermining evidence to the conclusion).

[3] Lehrer (1965).

Mary might be described as making all the following inferences. (1) She rejects her belief that no friend of hers owns a Ford. (2) In addition she comes to believe that one of her friends owns a Ford and accepts a story about Nogot. (3) As in (2), except that she accepts a story about Havit rather than one about Nogot. (4) She does all the preceding things. All the inferences (1)-(4) might be ascribed to Mary by an appropriate reasoning instantiator F (chapter three, section 6). Mary knows because inference (3) adds nothing false to her view.

Given Mary's antecedent beliefs, there is a single maximal inference she makes, (4), which is the union of all the inferences she makes. An inference is warranted only if it is included in the maximal warranted inference. That is why the lottery paradox does not arise even though we allow for the possibility that Mary makes more than one inference (section 2).

In order to handle the problem about premises we must require, not that the actual premises of the inference (everything Mary believes ahead of time) be known to be true but only that the inference remain warranted when the set of antecedent beliefs is limited to those Mary antecedently knows to be true and continues to know after the inference. More precisely, let (A, B) be an inference that rejects the beliefs in the set A and adds as new beliefs those in the set B; let $B \cup C$ be the union of the sets B and C, containing anything that belongs either to B or to C or to both; and let Φ be the empty set that contains nothing. Then principle P is to be replaced by the following principle P^*, which gives necessary and sufficient conditions of inferential knowledge.

$P*$ S comes to know that h by inference (A, B) if and only if (i) the appropriate reasoning instantiator F ascribes (A, B) to S, (ii) S is warranted in making the inference (A, B) given his antecedent beliefs, (iii) there is a possibly empty set C of unrejected antecedent beliefs not antecedently known by S to be true such that the inference $(\Phi, B \cup C)$ is warranted when antecedent beliefs are taken to be the set of things S knows (and continues to know after the inference (A, B) is made), (iv) $B \cup C$ contains the belief that h, (v) $B \cup C$ contains only true beliefs.

Reference to the set C is necessary to cover cases in which S comes to know something he already believes.[4] Part (v) of $P*$ captures what was intended by our original principle P.

6. Summary

Our previous conception of induction as inference to the best explanatory statement fell short in three ways. It failed to account for the rejection of previously held beliefs, it failed to avoid the lottery paradox, and it treated deduction as a form of inference. The last of these is especially serious since it can lead to misguided theories in response to a form of skepticism it encourages; and it can also suggest the construction of induc-

---

[4] Recall the case of Larry and Mabel described above (chapter two, section 3). Larry's inference concerning the bank manager gives him knowledge of his wife's innocence, although he has all along believed her innocent.

tive or practical logics, having to do with inductive or practical reasoning. These defects are avoided if induction is taken to be inference to the best total explanatory account. We can reject beliefs because the account we come to accept may not contain beliefs we previously accepted. Any inference we are warranted in making is included in the maximal inference we are warranted in making, so the lottery paradox cannot arise. Deductive arguments are not inferences but are explanatory conclusions that can increase the coherence of one's view.

Finally, all this means that principle P must give way to principle P^*, which says that we know by inference only if one of our inferences remains warranted and leads to the acceptance only of truths when restricted in premises to the set of things we know ahead of time to be true.

Chapter **11**

Inference in Perception

1. Direct perceptual knowledge based on inference

A friend, Jones, enters the room and you recognize him immediately. It seems natural to say that you do not need to infer that Jones has just come in, since you can directly see who it is. Even so your knowledge is based on inference.

If you are to know that Jones has come in, it is not enough that seeing him come in causes you to believe that he has come in. Your belief must be a reasonable one, and it is reasonable only if it is part of a reasonable conclusion, given your background beliefs along with information about how things look to you. Suppose that Jones has disguised himself to look like Smith. Expecting Jones leads you to think, "There is Jones," when he enters, even though if you thought about it for a moment you would think, "Wait! That's Smith, not Jones." In such a case, you do not come to know that Jones has come in. This makes sense because perception involves inference. You do not know because your inference was not warranted.

Suppose that Jones had come in undisguised but your background beliefs include the information that there is in the building someone who looks enough like Jones to be his double. Then, even though seeing Jones leads you to believe that Jones has just come in, you do not come to know this, since you are not warranted in believing it. This is so because the inference you made in coming to believe Jones had come in was not warranted.

Another indication that direct perception involves inference is that there are Gettier examples involving direct perceptual knowledge. If we suppose that direct perceptual knowledge is based on inference, these Gettier examples are easily accounted for. If we were to suppose that direct perceptual knowledge does not involve inference, these Gettier examples would require special treatment of an obscure sort.

Recall the following example. A man looks and comes to believe that there is a candle directly before him. There is a candle there; but a mirror intervenes to show the reflection of a candle actually off to one side. The man's belief is justified and true; but he does not know. If his belief is the result of inference, his failure to know is easy to understand. Since inference attempts to find the best total explanatory account, he infers an explanation of the way things look. He infers that it looks to him as if there were a candle before him because there is a candle there and because of the normal connection between the way things look and the way things are. Since that explanation is essential to his conclusion but is false, he does not come to know that there is a candle before him even though his belief is justified and true.

Supposing that his belief is based on inference allows this Gettier example to be explained in the same way that others are. If such a supposition were not made, it is doubtful that any account could be given of this and similar Gettier examples.

There are also Gettier examples involving direct perceptual knowledge that depend on the fact that the conclusion of an inference includes the claim that there is no undermining evidence to that conclusion that one does not possess (chapter four, section 3). For example, seeing Jones come into the room from the hall leads you to believe that Jones has come into the room, and you are justified in believing that. However, quite unknown to you there is also someone who looks enough like Jones to be his double. You cannot be said to know that Jones has come into the room because there is undermining evidence to your conclusion that you do not possess.

Another indication that perception involves inference comes from the psychology of perception. A person determines how far away a perceived object is by means of cues involving overlapping of surfaces and texture gradients. It is natural to describe this as a matter of inference: given these cues the perceiver infers that objects are in those places. The relevant cues make it reasonable to suppose the objects are where the perceiver infers they are. Suppose that two surfaces A and B present the following appearance:

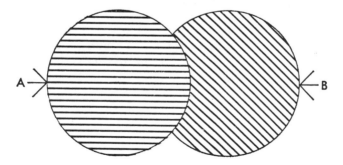

Ordinarily one would assume that A overlaps and is therefore in front of B. That assumption would ordinarily represent a warranted inference. If A and B are both circles and A is in front of B and slightly to its left, they would present that appearance. The hypothesis accounts for the way they look. On the other hand, if B is closer than A, B must have an irregular shape. Ordinarily it is more plausible to assume that B has a regular shape and is therefore behind A. Under special laboratory conditions, this reasoning might not be warranted; but ordinarily it is. So it is natural to ascribe it to the perceiver.

The inferences a perceptual psychologist ascribes to a perceiver are similar to those we would ascribe to him in order to account for Gettier examples, since they involve considerations concerning the best explanation of how things look. The two lines of argument, one from perceptual psychology, the other concerning the ordinary use of the word "know," reinforce each other and the conclusion that direct perceptual knowledge involves inference.

2. Inference in the ordinary sense?

Contemporary psychologists tend to view a perceiver as an information-processing mechanism, a kind of analog computer. Sensory stimulation serves as input which is processed in such a way that a representation of the surroundings is formed. Usually, the perceiver already has some representation of the surroundings; perception leads him to modify his representation. Now, it is natural to describe mechanical information-processing machines—like computers—as if they could calculate, figure something out, and infer conclusions. When the perceiver is conceived as an information-processing device, it becomes natural to describe him in the same way. Having extended the application of "inference" so that computers can be said to infer, it is natural to extend it so that perceivers are also said to infer.

For example, Gregory defends the attribution of unconscious inference to the perceiver in the following passage:

> Helmholtz spoke of perception in terms of "unconscious inferences." . . . At this point we must be clear that there is no "little man inside" doing the arguing, for this leads to intolerable philosophical difficulties. Helmholtz certainly did not think this, but his phrase "unconscious inferences," and his descriptions of perceptions as "unconscious conclusions" did perhaps suggest, at the time, to people unfamiliar with computers, some such unacceptable idea. But our familiarity with computers should remove temptation towards confusion of this kind. For we no longer think of inference as a uniquely *human* activity involving consciousness (p. 30).

Now, the fact that the ascription of inference to perceivers has a connection with its ascription to computers may suggest that a special technical sense of "inference" is relevant here. But I do not think so.

It is true that you will say, "I do not *infer* that Jones is here, I can *see* that he is." I have argued that emphasis in such sentences serves to indicate a "merely" as in "Nixon is not *an* elected official, he is the president" (chapter seven, section 1). The remark about belief and knowledge means, "I do not merely believe that Jones is here, I know that he is here." Similarly, your remark about inference and perception can be interpreted to mean, "I do not merely infer that Jones is here, I can see that he is here."

Furthermore, even if it should be true that most people do not believe that direct perceptual knowledge involves inference in the ordinary sense of inference, it does not follow that they are right. There is no reason to suppose that in presenting the argument above concerning Gettier examples concerned with direct perceptual knowledge I was introducing a new sense of "inference." Nor is there any reason to take the perceptual psychologist to be introducing a new sense of inference rather than discovering new facts about inference when he presents his theory of depth perception.

In extending the application of the word "inference" in this way, do we extend the meaning of the word or do we leave the meaning alone and simply change our views about when inference occurs? There is no general way to answer questions like that, since there is no real distinction between changing our view and only appearing to do so by changing the meanings of our words (chapter six, section 8).

We can also put the problem like this. Consider someone who accepts the arguments from Gettier examples and from depth perception. Does that person use the word "inference" in different senses when he applies it to direct perceptual knowledge and when he applies it to more ordinary cases? Here the burden of proof lies on someone who wishes to multiply senses.

The idea that "inference" is used in a special sense when applied to direct perception may derive from the view that inference in the ordinary sense is a conscious process. As we have seen in chapter two, section 2, the idea that we can be conscious of our reasons is plausible only for "deductive reasons" and not for "inductive reasons." Having made an inference, we are often in a position to produce a relevant deductive argument. But, as we have also seen in chapter ten, section 3, that does not imply that our inference was conscious. An argument in the relevant sense is not an inference in the relevant sense. It is at best part of the conclusion of an inference. Inference is never a conscious process, even though we are sometimes aware of part of the conclusion of an inference. Since inference is never conscious, the fact that inference in perception is unconscious does not mean that "inference" is here used in a special technical sense.

3. Sense data

When you see Jones in the room, light striking your eye stimulates your retinal nerve and begins a process that culminates in your belief that Jones is in the room. If it is granted that your belief is the result of inference, it is natural to suppose that the stimulation of the retinal nerve causes sensory experience which you then use as data for your inference. Stimulation of the retina causes it to look to you as if Jones is in the room. You then infer that it looks that way because Jones is in the room.

One problem with this is that some aspects of the way

things appear is determined by inference. For example, reasoning involving overlap, texture gradients, and perspective figures in the apparent location of objects. Inference gets into the story before it is completely determined how things look.

This suggests that there are two or more levels of visual experience. Perhaps at the basic level the world is represented in a two-dimensional array of apparent color shapes. At a less basic level the world appears as a three-dimensional structure of color volumes. And there are even less basic levels. For example, things can look as if they were moving. This is not just a remark about what we conclude about the things in question, since we may very well conclude that they are not really moving. The lights around certain theatre marquees seem to be moving but we know that they are not really doing so. Similarly, something can look cold, a face can look happy, a gesture can look threatening, and the defendant can look guilty.

A version of the original suggestion that allows for different levels of experience would suppose that retinal stimulation directly causes, without inference, a representation at the first level, a two-dimensional layout in color. Inference would convert that representation into a three-dimensional structure of color volumes. Consideration of several successive representations would lead one to infer a dynamic picture. Further inference would add coldness, happiness, threateningness, or guilt.

But this cannot be right. The various levels of experience are more interdependent than such a suggestion indicates. On any level, how things look depends on our views about how things are. There are many examples of this that seem to rule out the idea that how things look is built up level by level. Consider perception of language. We often make a guess about meaning and fill in the sounds or shapes to match that guess. Or consider this familiar sort of case. You seem to see Jones come in the door. On closer inspection, you see that it is Smith who looks nothing like Jones. You expected Jones but not Smith. Your beliefs and expectations affected the appearance and shape of the face you saw in an inferential way.

We can distinguish how things look from how we think they are, for sometimes these are distinct. How things look to a person represents a kind of sensory experience. But how things look is not just directly caused by sensory stimulation, since it is itself the product of inference. Furthermore, there does not seem to be any basic level of visual experience not itself the product of inference, and used itself as data for inference to how things look.

This raises several problems. What is sensory experience, if this is identified with how things look, sound, smell, feel, taste, etc.? Given that it results from inference, what is its connection with beliefs about the world that also result from inference in perception? And what serves as the data for this inference if there are no sense data in experience? I shall try to answer these questions in the rest of this chapter. In the next section I will consider what sensory experience is. After that I will come back to the question concerning the ultimate data of inference.

4. How things look

Just as your belief that Jones is in the room represents Jones as in the room, its looking to you as if Jones were in the room is a matter of your representing Jones as in the room. In either case you form a representation of Jones in the room. For that representation to be a belief is for it to function as a belief in your psychology—for you to treat it as a belief. When it looks to you as if Jones were in the room you are (to some extent) disposed to believe that Jones is in the room. You are disposed to let the representation you form of Jones in the room function as one of your beliefs. Ordinarily this disposition is not inhibited. Ordinarily when it looks to you as if Jones were in the room, you believe that he is in the room. Sometimes, however, special reasons intervene. In that case your disposition to belief may be inhibited and other beliefs may be accepted. The distinction between how things look and how you think they are is a distinction between how you are disposed to think they are and how you actually do think they are.[1] Of course, not every representation you are disposed to treat as a belief is a representation concerned with how things look. How things look is a matter of a certain kind of disposition to accept a certain kind of representation as one of your beliefs.

The representations involved in its looking to you as if Jones were in the room are not purely linguistic representations. Even an extremely detailed story cannot capture the sensuous richness of how things look. More generally, your conception of yourself and your sur-

[1] Pitcher.

182

roundings is not a purely linguistic story but involves other sorts of representations as well, even as it were a kind of map or picture of yourself in your surroundings.[2] How things look is constituted by a partly pictorial nonlinguistic representation of oneself in certain surroundings—a representation which you are (at least partly) disposed to treat as one of your beliefs.

From another angle, the difference between how things look and how you believe they are reflects a difference between automatic inferences and inferences that require some attention. Consider what happens when you are driving a car while talking to your passenger. If you are familiar with the route, you need not pay any attention to the driving. You can concentrate on the conversation. You have learned complex automatic responses that enable you to weave in and out of traffic, passing some cars, letting other cars go by, signalling for a turn, and switching lanes if there is too much traffic in the lane you are in, all this without ever taking your mind from the conversation. In these situations you make automatic inferences that are responsible for various choices. In other situations driving requires attention. If the road is unfamiliar, trusting your automatic responses can lead to missing the crucial turnoff. In such a case, relevant reasoning must be less automatic.

The way things look is the result of automatic inference of the sort we are used to making in visual perception. The distinction between how things look and how we think they are arises because a person does not always rely on automatic habits of inference but some-

2 Armstrong (pp. 209-211).

times pays attention and reaches relatively unusual conclusions. Notice that when a person is driving in the automatic way he responds directly to how things look, e.g., he slams on his brakes without thinking when he mistakes the moving shadow of a cloud for a child running out into the street. There is a difference between how things look and how we take them to be when we are not simply relying on such automatic habits and responses but are paying attention and consciously directing the show ourselves.

How things look is constituted by a representation that results from the automatic sort of inference. That explains why things continue to look other than they are long after we have become convinced they are other than they look. We retain the tendency to infer in the old way. On the other hand, our automatic inferences can be to some degree modified by practice, which is why a person wearing distorting spectacles that turn everything upside down eventually comes to see everything right side up. When he finally takes the glasses off everything then looks upside down because his automatic habits of inference have changed.[3]

5. Data

Direct perceptual knowledge is based on inference, but not just on inference from prior beliefs, since then there would be no connection with perception. Perception must give us data that are not themselves the result of inference but which permit the inference on which perceptual knowledge is based. The data cannot be pro-

[3] Pitcher (pp. 152-171).

vided by sensory experience, since that experience is constituted by representations which are themselves the products of inference of a more or less automatic sort. But then what could these data be?

I suggest that the data are the sensory stimulations that provide the input to the complex information processing system composed of brain and nervous system. Perceptual knowledge is based on inference from sensory stimulations. But this remark must be interpreted very carefully, for consider the following objection.

> The typical perceiver knows little psychology and nothing about stimulations of his retinal nerve. So, if data needed for his inference include claims about his sensory stimulation, he does not believe the data. But how can an inference from certain data be ascribed to someone if he does not believe the data? To so ascribe inference to someone would be to misuse our ordinary concept of inference. So, direct perceptual knowledge cannot be the result of inference from sensory stimulation if "inference" is used in anything like its ordinary sense.

In order to meet this objection, we must consider what is involved in the claim that perceptual inference is inference from sensory stimulation. This should not be interpreted to mean that the perceiver's inference rests on data that contains claims *about* sensory stimulation, for then the objection would go through, since the typical perceiver has no beliefs about sensory stimulation. The claim that perceptual inference is from sensory stimulations should rather be interpreted to mean that sensory stimulations serve for the perceiver

185

as representations that constitute the data for his inference. The data are not *about* sensory stimulations, they *are* sensory stimulations. Sensory stimulations serve the perceiver as nonlinguistic representations which cannot easily be put into words.

The stimulations of the perceiver's retinal nerve represent something for him in the way that input represents something for a computer. They have a role in some system of representation. Their representational characteristics derive from that system, a system that also admits of linguistic representations if the perceiver also has acquired a language. In order to be able to express in words the input data, we would have to know much more about the system of representation and its functioning than we know now. Even then it might be impossible to find linguistic representations equivalent to the nonlinguistic representations constituted by sensory stimulations.

6. Beliefs not based on inference

Different sorts of stimulation of his retinal nerve represent different things to the perceiver. The data of his inference include not the claim that his eye is being stimulated in one or another way but rather whatever is represented by that stimulation. Does he believe the data? He uses them in the way one uses beliefs in inference. So there is some reason to say that he believes them. It is true that the beliefs in question are ephemeral, since he quickly loses them. But that is to be expected of beliefs that say that something is happening *now*.

186

The beliefs thus constituting the data of perceptual inference are not themselves based on inference, and the same is true for many beliefs about your own psychological states. You can know that you believe that Jones is in the room without having to infer this from anything else. The same can be said of your knowledge that it looks to you as if Jones were in the room, as well as your knowledge that you wish Jones would leave. You know without inference that you have a headache and that your left foot itches.

Being in a given psychological state can lead you to represent yourself as in that state, where this representation is not a product of inference and where you are strongly disposed to let the representation function as one of your beliefs. However, other considerations may inhibit your disposition to treat as a belief the representation of yourself in certain psychological states. As a result you may prevent yourself from using the representation as a datum for further inference. For example, you may decide that you do not really desire what you seem to desire but really desire something else that you have trouble facing up to. In such a case you will attempt to overcome your inclination to treat as a belief the representation of yourself as having a particular desire.

So there is a sense in which your belief that you have a particular desire is not the product of inference and another sense in which it is. It is not in the sense that your representation of yourself as having that desire is not the product of inference. It is in the sense that inference could lead you not to treat that representation as one of your beliefs and therefore, presumably, could

187

lead you to treat it as one of your beliefs after all. This inference is relevant to whether you are justified in believing you have that desire.

Compare three cases. Its looking to you as if Jones is in the room involves a representation of yourself as in the room which is the product of automatic inference and to which nonautomatic inference can be relevant in deciding whether that representation will function as one of your beliefs. Your belief that you have a particular desire involves a representation which is not the product of inference but to which inference is relevant in deciding whether that representation will function as one of your beliefs. Finally, sensory stimulation of your sense organs constitutes a representation which is not the product of inference and to which inference is apparently not relevant in deciding whether it will function as one of your beliefs since it always functions in that way.

Chapter **12**

Inference in Memory

1. *Two views of memory*

Finally I want to suggest that knowledge of the past is based on reasoning concerning the best explanation of present memories. The best explanation of its seeming to you that certain things occurred in the past is that they did occur and you remember them. However, knowledge based on reasoning is based on actual reasoning (chapter two, section 3; chapter three, section 6); and it may seem implausible to suppose that you constantly reinfer all of your beliefs about the past from present memory data. It is true that, since inference is inference to the best total account, all your prior beliefs are relevant and your conclusion is everything you believe at the end. So, you constantly reaffirm your beliefs in inference. But it may seem wrong to treat inference as simply an inference from current memories to conclusions about the past since these conclusions were already accepted ahead of time.

Therefore, we might consider a different view of memory which does not treat it as a faculty for arriving at knowledge like reasoning or perception but takes memory to be the preserving of knowledge. If a belief is acquired and you continue to believe it, we speak of memory. On this second view, memory is not something

189

that makes such preservation of belief possible, but is rather the remembering itself, simply continuing to believe something.

I will argue that three considerations favor the inferential view of memory over the preservation view. One consideration is that if you are to continue to know it must remain rational to continue to believe as you do. The second consideration is that you can know something for a while until a point at which the knowledge is thereafter undermined by evidence you do not possess. We can make sense of these two considerations by adopting a version of the inferential conception of memory. Furthermore, the inferential conception seems to provide the only way to account uniformly for cases in which what you retain in memory is a present-tense statement like "Truman is the president."

2. *Irrationally continuing to believe something*

If memory were simply preservation of knowledge and belief, we might expect the following principle to be true.

If one comes to know something and continues to believe it, one continues to know it.

That is, we would expect knowledge to remain knowledge as long as one continues to believe as one does.

But suppose that the library detective knows that he saw Tom steal a library book. Tom's mother decides to invent some misleading evidence that she will present to the detective in order to destroy his knowledge. She goes up to him and tells him that Tom has an identical twin who was in the library at the time of the theft. Although her story is a complete fabrication, the detective believes what she says. However, being somewhat slow, he fails to see its relevance and continues to believe that he saw Tom steal the book. The detective came to know that Tom stole the book and he continued to believe it even after Tom's mother presented him with the phony evidence. But after the detective was presented with that evidence it was no longer true that he knew that Tom had stolen the book.

One does not continue to know something if it becomes irrational to continue to believe it. It is irrational for the detective to continue to believe as he does since he now has evidence that Tom may not have been the one who stole the book. The detective stops knowing even though he does not stop believing, so the suggested principle is false.

All this makes sense on the assumption that one constantly reinfers old beliefs. Given that assumption, if such an inference is no longer warranted, so that one should give up a belief, then the inference no longer gives one knowledge of the thing believed. Without such an assumption, the relevance of the rationality or irrationality of continued belief can be acknowledged only by means of an ad hoc modification of the originally suggested principle.

> If one comes to know something and continues to believe it, one continues to know it, provided that belief in it has not become irrational.

Even that much complication proves inadequate, however, because of the relevance of undermining evidence one does not possess.

3. Undermining evidence to memory knowledge

That undermining evidence one does not possess is relevant not just to the acquisition of knowledge but also to its maintenance is clear from the original example concerning Tom and the library detective. The detective knows that he saw Tom steal the book and so he testifies to the Judicial Council. After he leaves the hearing, Tom's mother fabricates her story about Tom's twin brother. Her lying testimony convinces the Judicial Council but is unknown to the detective back at his post in the library. It remains just as rational for him to continue believing as he does; but once Tom's mother has so testified, it is no longer true that the detective knows that Tom stole the book.

To account for this without supposing that continuing knowledge must be based on continuing reasoning, we would have to accept an even more complicated principle like this.

> If one comes to know something and continues to believe it, one continues to know it, provided that belief in it has not become irrational and there is no undermining evidence to it that one does not possess.

By itself such a principle is ad hoc and unilluminating. It does not reveal any connection between the rationality of coming to believe something and that of continuing to believe something, nor does it connect the role of evidence one does not possess in inference with its role in continuing to know something.

On the other hand, the inferential account of memory makes sense of all these things. Since inference is inference to the best total explanatory account, we reaffirm all our continuing beliefs in any inference. Sometimes inference leads us to delete something previously believed; sometimes it does not. Therefore, we may suppose that whenever we continue to believe something this is part of an inference to the best total explanatory account which does not delete the belief in question. That is, we may suppose that we are constantly inferring whatever we believe. Knowledge at any time is based on an inference made at that time. We lose knowledge if it becomes irrational to continue to believe as we do, since at that point the inference is no longer warranted. Evidence we do not possess is relevant, since we continually infer that there is no undermining evidence to our conclusion.

4. Continuing knowledge of the truth of tensed statements

Most citizens of the United States know who the president is. They know it without having constantly to think to themselves thoughts of the form "So and so is *now* president," and a moment later, . . . "So and so is *now* president." People remember who the president is. What they "store in memory" is a tensed statement which is constantly changing its reference to a particular time.

The inferential view of memory easily accounts for a continuing knowledge of the truth of tensed statements in exactly the way it accounts for other continuing knowledge. In continuing to accept a tensed statement, we infer it as part of inference to the best total explanatory account. Sometimes it is rational to delete a tensed statement from that account. In such a case we no longer know the statement is true even if we continue to accept it and it continues to be true. Consider, for example, someone in solitary confinement who continued to believe from 1947 through 1950 that Truman was the president of the United States, even though he had no information concerning the outcome of the election in 1948. After 1948 he could not be said to know that Truman was president.

A preservation theory of memory applied to tensed statements is obviously wrong when associated with the principle:

If one comes to know something and continues to believe it, one continues to know it.

If the belief in question is belief in a tensed statement, the principle can go wrong in the most blatant way, since after some time the tensed statement may become false. Even if it remains true, one does not know this in the absence of some reason to think it remains true. The constant-inference theory makes perfect sense of the facts concerning continuing knowledge of tensed statements. But the retention of this sort of knowledge is no different from the retention of knowledge of untensed statements. Therefore, the constant-inference theory should be accepted for all cases of memory and continuing knowledge.

References

D. M. Armstrong (1968). *A Materialist Theory of Mind.* Routledge and Kegan Paul. London.

A. J. Ayer (1969). *Metaphysics and Commonsense.* Macmillan. London.

D. C. Dennett (1969). *Content and Consciousness.* Routledge and Kegan Paul. London.

Keith Donnellan (1970). "Proper Names and Identifying Descriptions," *Synthese* 21.

Pierre Duhem (1906). *La Theorie Physique: Son Object et Sa Structure.* Paris.

Edmond Gettier (1963). "Is Justified True Belief Knowledge?" *Analysis* 23: 121-123.

Alvin Goldman (1967). "A Causal Theory of Knowing," *Journal of Philosophy* 64: 357-372.

Nelson Goodman (1965). *Fact, Fiction, and Forecast.* Harvard University Press. Cambridge, Mass.

R. L. Gregory (1970). *The Intelligent Eye.* McGraw-Hill. New York.

Paul Grice (1957). "Meaning," *The Philosophical Review* 64: 377-388.

C. G. Hempel (1965). *Aspects of Scientific Explanation and Other Essays in the Philosophy of Science.* Free Press. New York.

Jakobovits and Steinberg (1971). *Semantics.* Cambridge University Press. Cambridge.

David Kaplan (1969). "Quantifying In," *Synthese* 19: 178-214.

Jerold J. Katz and Jerry A. Fodor (1963). "The Structure of a Semantic Theory," *Language* 34: 170-210.

Saul A. Kripke (1972). "Naming and Necessity," in *Semantics of Natural Language* (Davidson and Harman, eds.) D. Reidel. Dordrecht.

Henry Kyburg (1961). *Probability and the Logic of Rational Belief*. Wesleyan University Press. Middletown.

George Lakoff (1971). "Generative Semantics." In Jakobovits and Steinberg (1971).

Keith Lehrer (1965). "Knowledge, Truth, and Evidence," *Analysis* 25: 168-175.

Keith Lehrer (1971). "How Reasons Give Us Knowledge, or the Case of the Gypsy Lawyer." *Journal of Philosophy* 68: 311-313.

Keith Lehrer and Thomas Paxson, Jr. (1969). "Knowledge: Undefeated Justified True Belief," *Journal of Philosophy* 66.

Isaac Levi (1967). *Gambling with Truth*. Knopf. New York.

George Pitcher (1971). *A Theory of Perception*. Princeton University Press. Princeton.

Paul Postal (1970). "The Surface Verb 'Remind,'" *Linguistic Inquiry* 1.

Hilary Putnam (1962). "It Ain't Necessarily So," *Journal of Philosophy* 59: 658-671.

W. V. Quine (1970). *Philosophy of Logic*. Prentice-Hall. Englewood Cliffs, New Jersey.

Colin Radford (1966). "Knowledge—By Examples," *Analysis* 27: 1-11.

F. P. Ramsey (1931). *The Foundations of Mathematics*. London.

Gilbert Ryle (1968). "A Puzzling Element in the Notion of Thinking," in P. F. Strawson (ed.) *Studies in the Philosophy of Thought and Action*. Oxford University Press.

Brian Skyrms (1967). "The Explication of 'X knows that p,'" *Journal of Philosophy* 64: 373-389.

Peter Unger (1967), "Experience and Factual Knowledge," *Journal of Philosophy* 64: 152-173.

Index

197

WITHDRAWN